CLASH OF THE COVENANTS

Escaping Religious Bondage
Through the Grace Guarantee

Michael C. Kapler

~ Dedication ~

Eternal thanks to my wife Jeanne, who has gracefully stood by me through all the hills and valleys of life over the decades with barely an argument between us. But apple is still better than cherry.

PREFACE

SOMEWHERE ALONG THE WAY, the question you will undoubtedly be asking is what my theological credentials are for writing a book about the subject of Bible covenants, God's grace, and the gospel. This is the point where the author will usually share their background touting educational degrees, extensive work in ministry, and possibly even their fishing license.

My story is a bit different. I haven't studied theology, I never attended Bible school, and I have no formal training in ministry. (Have I gained your confidence yet?) The road I have traveled allowed me to discover Jesus Christ in a very personal way, one that led me to what some may see as more unconventional forms of ministry.

Having spent much time in the Bible from an early age without being under any specific church teaching for many years, my faith and relationship with the Lord was very real to me and was not based upon religious tradition or denominational doctrine. I've always had a heart for people to know Jesus in an intimate way. My childhood was pretty normal, and I was far from perfect, but I was the kind of kid that would ask the teacher if I could go down the hall to get a drink of water so I could slip gospel tracts in the lockers of other students.

In my adult years when I began attending various churches, I picked up on many teachings that had common threads in spite of some differences in doctrine. I became a dedicated church attendee, making new friends along the way. Some of my friends and I would share the gospel with people on the street or at a local university. I spent nearly twenty years in

Christian radio broadcasting, playing music on the radio and encouraging people. It was fun and rewarding but also something we took very seriously, because when a phone call is received from someone who is suicidal with a bottle of pills in their hand, telling them you don't feel qualified to respond to their cry for help isn't why God had them call. We don't have the luxury of signing up for a training class when unexpected opportunities of ministry and helping others can occur at any time and place.

In recent years, I have co-hosted an online podcast where we receive tens of thousands of downloads each week. It has grown purely through word of mouth without donations, advertising, or paid promotion. We've received letters and correspondence from people all over the world thanking us for the gospel message we share and the impact it has had on them.

The point of all this is that most Christians aren't in full time ministry as an occupation, nor have the majority of us studied theology or even spent a lot of time in the Bible. Regardless of education or religious background, we can all begin to grasp a greater knowledge of biblical truths and reach some fascinating conclusions about God with the help, guidance, and revelation from the Holy Spirit. When we are able to put aside doctrines of tradition that have very little to do with the gospel and begin to see the good news for what it really is, we can experience God on a whole new level of freedom and love. The people I want to reach are the ones who have hungered for this kind of intimate relationship with God but have lacked the understanding or exposure to the revelation of its message.

Education is a fine thing, but don't let the religious establishment convince you that you're just the scarecrow from *The Wizard of Oz*, making you feel as though you have an inferior Bible brain because you are without some sort of certificate issued on a piece of paper. This isn't what qualified the apostles and believers in the early church, and it isn't what qualifies people today. The same Holy Spirit that we see move mightily in the lives of those in the pages of Scripture is the same Spirit living in believers today. *He has so much to share with us.*

This book wasn't meant to be a book at all. I started jotting down a few notes for an upcoming podcast about the Sermon on the Mount and something began to take over. Forty thousand words later, I began to realize I had entered into new territory called writing. It occurred to me along the way that I was learning some things I had not previously seen or heard that helped me connect to a better view of the gospel, and I felt compelled to share them.

Having a respectful discussion can be a good thing, but I'm not one who cares to argue or debate among the millions of opinions and viewpoints about the Bible. Whenever there is uncertainty in understanding various Scriptures, I prefer to gravitate in the direction of God's grace, while communicating the gospel of good news in order to help people discover that Christ has truly made them free. I have found that going any direction other than grace will lead to confusion, contradiction, and a sense of hopelessness. There has been a renewed wave sweeping the world with the message of God's unconditional, extravagant love and people are clearly desiring a deeper understanding of the grace guarantee.

Coming to a realization of the difference between the Old and New covenants and the power and freedom of the gospel of grace will likely bring a dynamic change to your life. Here is an example in a letter from someone who shared her experience with us after she first started listening to our "Growing in Grace" podcasts:

"I decided to play them in the background one day while I was cleaning my kitchen. By the third podcast, tears started to roll down my face. By the fifth podcast, I had abandoned my cleaning and was sobbing into my kitchen towel. The notion that I no longer had to perform for God or work to earn his pleasure was overwhelming, and something I longed for and knew I had to have. How ironic that I already had his forgiveness and complete acceptance all my Christian life, but never walked in it. Experience had taught me that trying not to sin and trying to perform for him were worthless, frustrating endeavors, but I just couldn't find freedom from a lifetime of bad, albeit well-intentioned teachings that said otherwise. Although I knew at some intellectual level that the Word didn't teach performance or the need to earn God's grace, it wasn't until I heard you teaching—out loud—what God's grace actually meant, that it clicked for me."

May it click for you too. God's blessings are yours.

INTRODUCTION

I WAS A YOUNG CHILD at the age of ten when I professed faith in Jesus Christ and I can remember it like it was yesterday. I recall looking over at the picture of Jesus hanging on my bedroom wall and coming to the realization that I had just entered into personal contact with the One represented in that picture. In that moment, I experienced something I can't describe, but the reality transpired within me that Jesus was more than a mere religion. He wasn't just a swear word or figment of someone's imagination, and he was much more than a picture on the wall.

Right after this experience, someone told me when I committed a sin I should simply remember to ask God for forgiveness and then I would be forgiven (again). They were sharing with me what had been handed down to them, but they said it rather nonchalantly and with a shrug, as if it wasn't a big deal. Naturally, I wanted to be forgiven, but just as importantly, I wanted to *stay* forgiven, so I figured I'd better stick to this rule. Little did I know it would eventually become one of the biggest burdens in my entire life. This small piece of well meaning instruction diminished the finished work of Jesus Christ and immediately placed the responsibility of my position with God back on my shoulders. Although I knew salvation was supposed to be a gift that brought freedom, I got it into my head that my release from prison would be based upon good behavior, while having to regularly report to my parole officer.

After more than two decades as a believer, I found myself at a spiritual crossroads. I became somewhat disconnected, disillusioned, disenchanted, or just plain "dissed" by much of the message I had been taught for so many years. Don't get me wrong—it wasn't that I was feeling challenged in my faith or doubting God. I could not deny his reality in my life, but I began to perceive that some of the status quo teaching and certain traditional beliefs commonly found in much of Christianity was inconsistent. Something was "off" and just seemed out of order. I began to see where certain things within traditional Christian concepts were not calculating correctly. I couldn't quite put my finger on all of it, but once I started doing the spiritual math, something was not adding up. I knew God's Word was truth, but much of what was being taught by the majority of churches and other popular ministries was somewhat contradictory at times. It brought me to a place where I felt like throwing in the towel when it came to "organized religion."

Puzzled by this overwhelming sense of frustration, I began to see the hypocrisy in much of the message being taught, including some of what I had shared with others over the years. It became more clear to me that many of the biblical dots did not connect the way they should, at least not with the way religion embraced them. As my frustration and burning dissatisfaction increased, I sensed God was somehow a part of why I was feeling this way. My heart knew it, but my mind could not put it together.

Through a series of circumstances, a moment came along where something started to click within and I was changed forever. I began to see the gospel and the entire Bible in a way that I had not seen it before. I became more aware that something powerful was missing from the message that most of us were hearing. Significantly, God began to open the vault to where many of the answers to my questions had been hidden. No, I didn't understand it all right away, but while at this crossroads, my eyes became opened to something that I had not fully seen after all those years as a believer—it was the gospel of grace!

I know this may sound ridiculous to some in the church world. Of course the gospel is about grace, right? Most institutional churches think it's a good topic to discuss, at least on special occasions. Everybody knows it has a sweet sound and causes the blind to see, because the hymn says it's so. But as I began to realize the *essence* of grace, it revealed a gospel thoroughly separated from religious rules and the effort of self-improvement. To my amazement, it was something that was noticeably absent from the typical teaching you would find in church or on TV and radio.

After a decade of growing in the grace of the gospel together, my friend Joel Brueseke was encouraged to launch an Internet podcast and asked me to co-host what would come to be known as "Growing in Grace." In time, Joel and I came to be criticized in a book full of legalistic attacks on some well known and respected ministries of God's grace. How our humble little podcast made the honorable mention list, I'll never know. We were accused of running from the words of Jesus. Nothing could be further from the truth. While this writing is not meant to be a specific response to that, the desire is to address a modern-day works message that has contributed to nullifying the promise of faith and the message of the gospel of grace. I believe the biggest culprit is the entanglement of two covenants that have clashed in the church.

Although there is plenty to ponder in these pages, what has been written is meant to be simple enough for a child to understand. Frankly, that's the only way I'm able to absorb the incredible depth of the gospel. Although no one has cornered the market on truth, in general, a hefty portion of what religion has put on display has caused many of us to misinterpret the good news. If I'm allowed to be less diplomatic, *we have been duped.* I'm not in the convincing business, I have no hidden agenda or denominational banner to wave, and I'm not even trying to persuade you to believe everything the same way I believe. I do not speak the language of a seminarian, and it is not my intention to negatively target any specific brand of dogma, denomination, or ministry by name. I simply want to offer some perspective that may help you begin to see the gospel in a different light and realize the love of God as you never have before.

If the closest thing to experiencing unconditional love has been from your pet dog, you've been missing out on something very special between you and your Creator.

CONTENTS

Preface...1

Introduction 5

Part 1: Covenant Confusion 9

(1) Bible Jeopardy: Questions to the Answers 10

(2) A Covenant Concoction...21

(3) The Law: Mission Impossible..33

(4) Written in Stone: The Ministry of Death..49

Part 2: Covenants Collide 66

(5) The New Testament Dividing Line..67

(6) The Insurmountable Sermon on the Mount..74

(7) The Lord's Prayer 87

(8) The Narrow Gate (The Sermon Concludes) 104

(9) Jesus: Good Cop, Bad Cop 112

(10) The Prodigal Chronicles (The Lost Son Unmasked) 125

Part 3: Covenant Conclusion..134

(11) The Forgiveness Business 135

(12) The Sin Confession Obsession...150

(13) Curse Free (Unless You Don't Tithe?) 170

(14) Grace Giving 179

(15) Changing Your Thinking (Repentance) 188

(16) Life in the New Covenant...198

(17) A New Creation 209

Epilog 221

About the Author..226

PART 1: COVENANT CONFUSION

Before getting started, I want to caution you in advance. *Reader discretion is advised.* I may put a few significant dents into some of the beliefs and traditions you have held most sacred, but my hope is to bring a newfound freedom and peace that will make the reality of joy more complete in your life.

Part 1 Overview:

A. It's about the context, not just the verses.
B. Acknowledging some of the differences between the Old and New Covenants.
C. The purpose of the law given to Israel in the first covenant, and why the law has no place in the life of a believer in Christ.

(1) BIBLE JEOPARDY: QUESTIONS TO THE ANSWERS

O NCE UPON A TIME in a land not so far away, there was a Christian who often wondered if God was disappointed with him for fear of not living up to certain expectations. The persistent apprehension as to where he stood with God followed him around like a dark shadow. Pecking away at his conscience were feelings of guilt resulting from inconsistencies with his behavior and a false sense of alienation and separation. Perhaps it was because of not reading the Bible more often, skipping church attendance, or spending excessive amounts of time with video games and watching television. At times, the claws of condemnation would grip his mind for other reasons, such as not giving and volunteering enough, wishing he could take back hurtful things he'd said or done, and regrets about relationships that had gone sour. Some of his struggles were more intense, such as not being able to shake specific sins or addictions, and his feelings of remorse for past failures of wrongdoing would sometimes just keep repeating themselves, no matter how hard he tried to improve.

Many of us can see ourselves in that scenario, at least in part. Regardless of our personal experiences and background in this life, most of us have sought to work at doing (or avoiding) certain things to make ourselves more acceptable to God. Humankind has pursued this path since

Adam and Eve, and whether it's realized or not, this also applies to people who have had very little interest or exposure to church, religion, or belief in a Supreme Being. In spite of our best and most sincere attempts, the results of human effort working to pursue favor with Almighty God will lead to fear and uncertainty. It often brings people to a place where they would rather just hide in the bushes instead of having to face their Creator in shame. Anyone who is caught in the quicksand of doing anything in order to attain right standing with God will persistently be haunted by the following questions: *What must I do? How much is enough? What am I lacking?*

Legalism and the Bible

Although the word *legalism* does not appear in Scripture, the concept is found extensively throughout. It can be viewed as a works-based religion built upon rules, regulations, or dos and don'ts that are meant to lead to salvation or securing favor with God. The results of legalism will lead to fear, accusation, disapproval of others, hypocrisy, a sense of worthlessness, despair, frustration, and guilt, just to name a few.

Legalism takes on many forms. As a young child eager to learn more about God, I picked up a discipleship book for new believers from the bookstore. It taught me I should share the gospel with at least three people each day, either verbally or by using what were called gospel tracts, in printed form. Naturally, the publisher just happened to sell these recommended tracts. I was also instructed to read ten chapters of the Bible every day without fail. It suggested that anything less *would be* a failure. So I took the advice of that spiritual legal counsel, and this new requirement I had established for myself became law to me. It didn't always matter how much I understood regarding what I was reading, as long as I made every attempt to meet the desired quota. If I fell short, I assumed God was disappointed with me, and falling short is what we humans do best. Reading only seven chapters could feel like a letdown. I would try to make up for it the next day, but you can probably figure out how that ended up over the long haul.

Like many believers, I had developed the desire to perform in a way that I perceived would be pleasing to God. But I was always starting over, trying again and falling short of whatever imaginary goal I thought God intended for me to achieve. This didn't apply to just Bible reading, but various aspects of what I thought were meant to be a part of the life of a believer. I hadn't yet realized this was the very thing Jesus came to deliver us from.

Having the desire to please God is a good thing, but we don't achieve this through a process of our own works and efforts; we do it through a different source known as faith—the kind of faith that works through love. Don't confuse "pleasing God" with whether he accepts you. You've already been accepted.

Since most people do not have a solid foundation of the gospel of grace, they are easily persuaded by various forms of legalism being poured into them over a period of many years. They have little or no idea they have been exposed to it, similar to asbestos poisoning hidden inside their own walls. They are programmed to think a certain way about God and the Bible, and it's a big challenge for people to change their thinking, especially when much of what they've been told has been held onto as a sacred and personal part of their belief system. Grace seems too easy. It sounds too good to be true, right? There *must* be more to it! They'll plead for teaching that is more centered on them, asking, "*How can I be a better servant? Tell me what I need to do instead!*"

Someone once said the Bible can be one of the most dangerous books you'll ever read—*if you don't understand the gospel.* While that sounds radical, we can plainly see the thousands of religions and cults that have developed, and most of them did it by using the Bible as their launching pad. We proclaim the Bible to be God's written Word and that it is truth, but what happens when a single verse is taken out of context and applied inaccurately? I've had people show up at my door who didn't claim Christ as Savior, and although they were quoting some of the same Bible verses I use, they had an entirely different message and agenda. It's not just the truth that makes us free, but as Jesus said, it's *knowing* the truth. God wills not only for all people to be saved, but to come to the knowledge of the truth (see 1 Timothy 2:4).

Our Source of Life

What is the reason or purpose for those who take time to read the Bible? Many of us have thought it is a requirement from God. Others turn to it for inspiration or to seek guidance on what they should do. Some think it provides nourishment to our inner being, and without it we would starve spiritually if not ingested on a regular basis. If we're being honest, most would say they are easily bored with the Bible. After all, this is common when it comes to something that seems hard for us to understand. It is often considered to be a single book when in fact it is made up of multiple books written by numerous people over an expanse of hundreds and even thousands of years. I'm going to make another radical statement that will raise some eyebrows, but will make more sense as we move forward, so try not to inhale too sharply. *Our source of life is not found in the pages of the Bible, but through the person of Jesus Christ.*

Please don't misinterpret what I'm saying, I have no intention of diminishing the truth that is found in the written pages; I cherish the Scriptures and cite them frequently. When it comes to using the phrase, *the Word*, most will automatically think of the written Word. However, the Word is more than just pages in something we call the Bible, because the Scriptures have been given to reveal the person of Jesus Christ. The reality is this—the living Word was around long before what was written:

> "In the beginning was the Word, and the Word was with God, and the Word was God. He was in the beginning with God. All things were made through him, and without him was not any thing made that was made. In him was life, and the life was the light of men. And the Word became flesh and dwelt among us, and we have seen his glory, glory as of the only Son from the Father, full of grace and truth" (John 1:1-4, 14).

The Word isn't just a book but is living and powerful, and can be found in the person of Jesus Christ himself. For many centuries after the cross, believers did not have Bibles on the shelf to read. If this collection of books is our lifeline to experiencing God on a daily basis, how did those people survive on a spiritual level? What about people around the world today who don't have access to these writings? As Jesus said to some Jewish people gathered around him:

"You search the Scriptures because you think that in them you have eternal life; and it is they that bear witness about me, yet you refuse to come to me that you may have life" (John 5:39-40).

On many occasions, we have elevated the "good book" above the person to whom the writings bear witness. We can be filled with all kinds of Bible information, but our origin of life is found only in the person of Jesus Christ and no other religious source or activity is able to provide it. Hearing truth may trigger faith, but the source of faith is found in Christ, who *is* the Word.

The notion that God would be disappointed in me if I didn't pray or read the Bible more frequently seems silly to me now. The Scriptures were meant for my benefit, not to satisfy a demanding homework assignment from him that did not exist. Contrary to what others may say, God's written Word is not meant to be an "instruction manual" to make you a better person, nor will you starve spiritually if you don't read it. In the past, I often viewed the Bible as a book that was there to remind me of my failures, and there were many days I would reluctantly pull it off the shelf to discover it weighed as much as a heavy barbell meant for a bench press. Have you ever been there?

Once we gain a better understanding of the gospel under the New Covenant, we'll be able to look at the Scriptures for the enjoyment of it. As we begin to see the big picture of what God did on our behalf, those pages will become nothing but good news. It is profitable for us, and will teach by correcting our wrong thinking about the gospel. It will train us in God's righteousness, not our own.

For Better or Verse

When it comes to memorizing Scripture, most of us have been trained to think in terms of verses. This isn't always a bad thing, except we need to regularly consider the bigger picture of context. *Context* is simply a thought or verbiage that surrounds words or a passage and can throw light on what it means. That which precedes or follows what is written can involve a connection that should not be ignored. While context may be overstated, you can't afford to overlook it, and it will be a primary theme for us from this point forward. Sometimes we get so caught up with staring at those individual verses that we miss their true meaning by not connecting with what surrounds them. Indeed, there is a bigger picture to be seen and understood, and it is a thing of beauty.

Rarely will we come to the knowledge of the truth from a single Bible verse without the context surrounding it. Chapters and verses were added for reference purposes, but at times we make the error of assuming an entire thought is placed inside of a single verse. It's like reading a headline without getting the full story. The Apostle Paul would sometimes take chapters (not just verses) to illustrate or emphasize a main point. Books such as Romans, Galatians, and Ephesians are great examples, as is the book of Hebrews.

Bible verses are often used by church people as though they were pieces of a jigsaw picture puzzle. You might think the pieces would be required to fit perfectly in order to create the picture, but such is not the case. It's not difficult to cut and paste verses of Scripture together to fit a particular mindset, assumption, or point of view. Simply pull enough verses out of context, make them appear to be in sync, and you'll be able to create a picture of *some* kind. Much like those connect-the-dot puzzles we played as children, as long as you can at least make it *look* like the dots are connected in the right order, you can draw whatever picture you want. People don't always look very closely and are easily misled, leaving them feeling puzzled and confused. Stare at the picture long enough and maybe you'll think you see the face of Jesus hidden in there somewhere.

We should not only consider the context of the passage, but *also the context of the gospel.* We find ourselves staring at the trees (verses) next to us, but there is an entire forest to be seen when viewed from the right perspective. It's okay to look at the scenery up close, and it's enjoyable to experience being on the mountain, but it can be even more majestic to step back and see the view of that mountain from a distance or to go to the top and observe the roads that lead to it. Regarding the two covenants, we have often missed out on the view of the forest or the reality of the bigger picture.

Here is one example of a tree up close: "For it is not the hearers of the law who are righteous before God, but the doers of the law who will be justified" (Romans 2:13).

Compare that verse with another tree from the Apostle Paul in the very next chapter: "For we hold that one is justified by faith apart from works of the law" (Romans 3:28).

So which is it? Are we justified by doing what the law demands, or is it *apart* from the law that we are made righteous? What may appear as a contradiction with those two trees is surrounded by the context of a landscape featuring beautiful scenery with a view that can be easily overlooked. In the second chapter of Romans and most of the third chapter, Paul was exposing the hypocrisy of self-righteous people by explaining how the Mosaic law required those who were under it to obey everything without failing. Those under the law would often judge others for the very things they didn't uphold themselves, and it caused "God's name to be blasphemed" among the Gentiles. The Jew was condemned by the law, and Gentiles without the law were also found guilty through their own conscience.

A "doer of the law" wasn't a person giving it their best shot; it was someone who followed it *to perfection.* Those who might have been considered the best of the bunch and recorded a significant portion of the Old Testament, were known to be adulterers and murderers. This hardly sounds like the qualifications of someone applying for the position of "law doer." A doer of the law had never been found until Jesus came along, which is why Paul goes on to clarify the change found in the New Covenant ... justification would have to arrive through a different source other than the law. All of us have fallen short of perfection, whether born from inside or outside of the Jewish race. Paul would take the rest of the book of Romans to reveal how deliverance from the law of *works* came through Jesus Christ, and brought us the *gift* of God's righteousness.

Think of Bible verses as tiny little dots or pixels that make up a picture. If you get too close to the image, it will be blurry and distorted. As we step back for a clearer view, we'll discover the entire Bible is really a picture of Jesus Christ. What are often considered as "topics" for discussion or sermon material in the religious realm, are actually things found and contained in the person of Jesus. Whether it be righteousness, grace, peace, life, forgiveness, the Word, the covenant, the kingdom ... Jesus is the personification of these and much more. Any gospel discussion without the centerpiece of Christ and the finished work of the cross is just meaningless bloviating.

Religion and Double Jeopardy

You'll notice I will often refer to the word *religion* and usually in the negative sense. Basically, I see it as a form of legalism, where people are trying to do something to get a response from God instead of resting in his response to us. Even after years of inflation, religions are still just a dime a dozen because they all follow the same basic path—the undertaking of outwardly performing in a way that will hopefully make them more acceptable to their creator. This thing we call Christianity was meant to be separated from that pack of wolves by God demonstrating his love through Jesus Christ, and through him did *everything* necessary to bring us into a state of perfection.

The waters are a bit murky when it comes to defining the actual meaning of the word "religion." Language experts will differ, but many believe the English version of the word appears to stem from the Latin word *religare*, which means "to bind." This can suggest "to place an obligation on" or possibly "a bond between humans and gods." Since our English word was derived many centuries later, there is no clear word in the (Old Testament) Hebrew that translates into the word *religion*, and it would be rare to find in English Bibles. In the New Testament, there are just a few appearances of the word, even though the English translations don't match clearly with the Greek language. *Threskeia* means "worship of the gods, as expressed in ritual acts" (Strong's G2356). This is especially from an external and ceremonial practice, and can be applied in a very generic sense.

My point with this is that religion can mean many different things when it comes to how people are bound to a particular belief system, and how they relate to their god or supreme power. The practice of some sort of religious, outward ritual or expression can originate from many sources, whether good, bad or ugly. Being "religious" can apply to anyone, and this isn't necessarily a title that we should want to be identified with, nor should it define who we are in Christ.

Over the years, I've seen many people hurt by *Christian religion*. These are victims who walk away from the institutional church dazed and confused, feeling the need to get the lead out, not wanting anything to do with it any more. It's not so much that these people are angry with God; more than likely they think God is angry with them (he isn't). Most people who leave the church institution are perceived as walking away from the Lord, but truth be told, they may just be departing from the wrong message. Some of the victims are even ministers themselves.

It saddens me to say that I've seen far too many people subscribe to the religion of atheism, all because of the negative and judgmental treatment they received from self-righteous church people. If you're one of those who feels like a casualty of Christianity, stick with me, because I hope to see you free from whatever bondage or pain that you've been pierced with as a result of hollow religion. After all, placing your hope in "nothing" isn't going to be your answer.

In our modern entertainment culture, *Jeopardy!* is known as a popular television game show that features a quiz competition in which contestants are presented with general knowledge clues in the form of answers and must phrase their responses in question form. Imagine the difficulty in trying to come up with the correct question if you were given the wrong clue or wrong answer. The word "jeopardy" can be defined as an exposure to loss, harm, death, or injury. It can also mean the danger of being found guilty, resulting in punishment.

Have you ever felt as though your spiritual life was in jeopardy? There came a time in my Christian life when I found myself trying to ask the right questions, but I was unknowingly doing it from a mindset of having the wrong answers to start with. I hear it from people all the time—asking questions that are coming from a framework built upon a foundation related to misunderstandings about the gospel. This is a big challenge, because many of these things have been learned over a lifetime, hidden within the cracks and crevices of our minds.

Although I've now spent many years exposed to the gospel of unlimited grace and unconditional love, I still find myself in a constant place of needing to *unlearn* from years of traditional misinformation. I'm not blaming religion entirely; after all, I bought into much of what is taught.

But until we have a complete paradigm shift from certain assumptions that have led us astray, we'll be left with confusion and a sense of anxiety. While it may be a jungle out there, the questions to the answers are asked from within. Our answers to the questions will arrive in the same way. In this book journey, we will occasionally pause to ask a question that is based upon answers given to us from the gospel. They are designed to provoke thought, exercise common sense, and help to transfer our thinking to an entirely different paradigm than what the religious business has sold to us.

As a former broadcaster, it was a habit to make sure I would be heard by checking my microphone. The scientific approach to this was by talking into it prior to recording by saying something like "Testing 1, 2, 3." Let's begin with a little microphone test of our own so I can check to make sure you are hearing me. This "test of the testaments" is a short list of thoughts related to concepts many of us have been taught regarding Christianity and God and the Bible. As you look at these, determine whether they resonate *accuracy* or *error* with you:

- The New Covenant is an addition to the existing Old Covenant.
- We should try to live by the Ten Commandments.
- Yielding to temptation means you have fallen from grace.
- Everything Jesus said was meant for you personally.
- If you don't forgive others, then God won't forgive you.
- Sin will hinder our fellowship with God and may cause a separation.
- You must confess all your sins to be forgiven.
- You will be blessed if you tithe, but cursed if you don't.
- You need to repent of your sins for salvation.
- The Holy Spirit convicts you of your sins.

If any of these sounded more true than false, the goal will be to bring you to a place where you will experience a complete change of mind, thereby avoiding any chance of *double jeopardy.* You shouldn't have to go through another judgment for something when you've already been declared innocent of the crime.

Whatever you've experienced in terms of spiritual jeopardy, despair, guilt, and condemnation, those things are about to be permanently sent to a place known as *once upon a time.* It's a land far, far away never to be remembered or revisited again. Get ready for some good news.

(2) A COVENANT CONCOCTION

I N THE CHRISTIAN CHURCH WORLD, there has been a significant misunderstanding or lack of knowledge regarding the two primary covenants in the Bible. While it's true God did make various covenants with different men in the Old Testament, basically it's pretty simple regarding the covenants made with the house of Israel. We have:

A: The Old Covenant
B: The New Covenant

A covenant is defined as a will, a testament, or an arrangement between two parties (Strong's G1242). We find the word *covenant* is sometimes translated as *will* or *testament* in Scripture. Since a covenant is generally agreed upon between two parties, it's important for us to realize God did not force the Old Covenant with the Mosaic law down the throat of Israel. They knew what the law stated and they agreed to it. In spite of all that God did to deliver them out of Egypt, they were ignorant enough to sign on to an arrangement where blessings would depend upon *their* faithfulness instead of simply trusting in God's faithfulness towards them. Pride and arrogance took center stage when they said, "All that the LORD has spoken we will do" (see Exodus 19:7-8). In essence, this was code for trusting in themselves and their own ability. Eventually, we'll see why they would've been better off saying, "We can't do this!"

What do you suppose would win the award for bringing the most confusion about the true meaning of the gospel than anything else? One consideration that should be put on the nomination list is the mistake of mixing portions of these two covenants together and producing doctrines equivalent to a Christian casserole or "gospel goulash." Unfortunately, this has been a foundational aspect of many church teachings. Since believers consider the Scriptures to be God's written Word, it is often assumed that nearly everything within both covenants is meant for them in a direct, personal way. However, a mixed concoction of the two covenants together will lead to a diluted message of what was accomplished for us at the cross. These covenants are not like a chocolate peanut butter cup, as if they are two great tastes that go great together. In fact, they are more like orange juice and toothpaste (don't even try it). By themselves, each covenant had a purpose, but the reason they aren't meant to be mingled is because they provided ingredients that are on the opposite end of the spectrum—one covenant brought death and the other brought life. Quite often the starting point for covenant confusion is not realizing the Old was made obsolete, removed completely, and replaced with something New.

We have been drilled with phrases such as *Judeo-Christian* that have caused us to jumble one covenant with the other, as if they were meant to be merged together as one. This combination of law and grace has transpired into something I'll call *legalanity*. We've been trying to put a square peg into a round hole and the pieces simply don't fit unless they are altered. It's no wonder we've struggled in understanding the basic foundation of the gospel or our new identity in Christ. It will be difficult to effectively communicate truth to the unbelieving world when we're sending them mixed signals that may as well be in Morse code.

Religionists who blend together the two covenants love to pull the ol' bait-and-switch. They'll offer forgiveness for free and then reveal exceptions in the fine print later, including tax, title, and license. This results in people ending up in despair as they try to make payments for something they'll never be able to afford. We can be freed from this by having our minds renewed to the gospel. Throwing the Bible into a blender and combining ingredients that clash with each other will bring a bitter taste, leaving us to thirst for something better. It's time to check the expiration date on what we've been drinking ... the pure and everlasting New Covenant of Jesus Christ is our solution.

While the New Covenant needed to be made with someone who would be born of a woman on planet earth, this time the covenant being made with the house of Israel would come through One that wouldn't fail. Unlike previous covenants made between God and his people, the brilliance on the part of God with the New is that he would make it with someone besides you and me. If there is one thing I could suggest that you keep on your mental shelf for easy access, it is that *Jesus Christ* is our guarantee, not our attempts at obedience, performance, or effort. As it says in Hebrews 7:22 (NASB), "Jesus has become the guarantee of a better covenant." This covenant is not something you and I are going to break, fail, or forfeit, because Jesus is the mediator that ensures the validity of the new and better arrangement:

> "But as it is, Christ has obtained a ministry that is as much more excellent than the old as the covenant he mediates is better, since it is enacted on better promises" (Hebrews 8:6).

When compared to the first covenant ushered in through Moses, we have something that is more excellent, which literally means different. It is better and it has been established on better promises.

Meet the New Boss—Not Like the Old Boss

Let's take a look at the introduction to the New Covenant as foreseen by the prophet Jeremiah and explained in the context of Christ by the writer of Hebrews:

> "For if that first covenant had been faultless, there would have been no occasion to look for a second. For he finds fault with them when he says: 'Behold, the days are coming, declares the Lord, when I will establish a new covenant with the house of Israel and with the house of Judah, not like the covenant that I made with their fathers on the day when I took them by the hand to bring them out of the land of Egypt. For they did not continue in my

covenant, and so I showed no concern for them, declares the Lord' " (Hebrews 8:7-9).

There would've been no need for a different covenant if the first one had been successful. However, the covenant wasn't the problem; it was with the people where fault was found. Observe carefully when God said this new covenant would not be anything like the first one, so we know that something different is being brought into play. I repeat, *it would not be like the first covenant.* The passage continues:

> "For this is the covenant that I will make with the house of Israel after those days, declares the Lord: I will put my laws into their minds, and write them on their hearts, and I will be their God, and they shall be my people. And they shall not teach, each one his neighbor and each one his brother, saying, 'Know the Lord,' for they shall all know me, from the least of them to the greatest. For I will be merciful toward their iniquities, and I will remember their sins no more.
> "In speaking of a new covenant, he makes the first one obsolete. And what is becoming obsolete and growing old is ready to vanish away" (Hebrews 8:10-13).

For those who believe certain elements of the Mosaic law are still meant for us today, they like to point out from the above passage that God would write his laws on their hearts. The writer of Hebrews tweaked Jeremiah's quote just the least little bit by using the phrase "my laws" and not *my law.* This is crucial to understand because the previous covenant had a package known as *the Law.*

Realizing the second covenant would not be like the first, we can conclude this is not speaking about the law of Moses on our hearts, but something different. Why? For one thing, even Gentiles outside of the Jewish race who did *not* have the law, already had the works of the law written on their hearts (see Romans 2:14-15). When they instinctively did the things of the law, though not having the law, they became a law to themselves with their conscience bearing witness while having conflicting thoughts, either accusing or excusing them. The work of this law could not justify and is not what is written on our hearts in a new and better covenant.

There are hundreds of references which reflect back on "the law" in the New Testament, but only twice do we find mention of God's *laws* (plural). These are found in the passage above, and it is repeated in the tenth chapter of Hebrews, revealing the new covenant of Christ. So if it's not the old law of Moses written on our hearts, what is the writer talking about in relation to the New Covenant? In the book of Romans, Paul referred to the *law of the Spirit of life* and the *law of faith*. These "new" laws replaced the law of commandments from the previous covenant. We have been transferred into an entirely different system than what the Jewish people were connected to in the first covenant. James called it the *law of liberty*:

> "For whoever shall keep the whole law, and yet stumble in one point, he is guilty of all. For He who said, 'Do not commit adultery,' also said, 'Do not murder.' Now if you do not commit adultery, but you do murder, you have become a transgressor of the law. So speak and so do as those who will be judged by the law of liberty. For judgment is without mercy to the one who has shown no mercy. Mercy triumphs over judgment" (James 2:10–13 NKJV).

Observe how James contrasted the law of Moses with the law of liberty. Under the first covenant, if one could manage to perfectly keep 612 rules, but stumbled at good ol' number 613, they would be declared guilty of breaking the entire law, because it was a package deal. Imagine if it really *were* the law of Moses written on our hearts with hundreds of commands. Yikes! This would mean all the Jewish customs and regulations would still be in play, such as the many Sabbath rules, not to mention the dietary commands, wardrobe restrictions, and so much more. Common sense should tell us these are not what have been written on our hearts inside of our current covenant, which is better and unlike the first one. This would place us back into the same system that Israel was under, which was purposely designed to be overwhelming with the result of underperforming. Under the law of the Old Covenant, judgment won't show mercy (compassion) to those who haven't shown mercy, but now under the law of liberty, mercy triumphs over judgment.

The Apostle Peter stated to the leadership at the church in Jerusalem that the former covenant of the Mosaic law was a heavy yoke "that neither we nor our fathers have been able to bear" (Acts 15:10). However, the Apostle John said something that appears to be quite different in his epistle:

> "There is no fear in love, but perfect love casts out fear. For fear has to do with punishment, and whoever fears has not been perfected in love. We love because he first loved us. For this is the love of God, that we keep his commandments. *And his commandments are not burdensome*" (1 John 4:18-19, 5:3). *Italics added.*

Compare what John just said to the Apostle Peter's statement about the Mosaic law and commandments being a burden the Jewish people were unable to bear. Did Peter and John have an honest disagreement which led to a contradiction in Scripture? Of course this is not the case, because they were simply referring to commandments from different covenants. Under the command of the Mosaic law, even the attempt to love God with all of one's might and to love others was a yoke of bondage, but under the current covenant *in Christ*, loving God and loving each other is not burdensome because it occurs freely apart from the requirement. Whereas the old way brought conditions leading to bondage and fear, the new way has brought love and acceptance, and allows us to love God and others because we now realize his love for us. The "law of liberty" under the New Covenant is never burdensome and always brings love, life, grace and mercy.

Don't Think Too Hard

Theologians are divided on whether there is currently one covenant or two. Some have the view there was no end to the Old and the New is simply a different application or administration of the first one. Other religious scholars may argue the New Covenant was to be made with the house of

Israel and they haven't yet accepted the terms of the agreement. Jesus made it clear that Israel's rejection would not hold back the will of God, because the new arrangement would *not* be made with fallen man, but with the Messiah who would represent Israel as the mediator. The "agreement" would simply be to believe in Christ, and part of the mystery that would be revealed after the cross is that Gentiles would also be invited into the house.

During his ministry on earth, Jesus said that he was sent only to the lost sheep of the house of Israel. As we consider the context of what Jesus was ministering while the Old Covenant was still in effect, we can now look back and conclude that salvation would not be offered to Israelites only. However, some covenant clashing theologians have applied that type of logic on the subject of the New Covenant, where our salvation is contained. In other words, if we're still waiting for the end of the first covenant in order for the second one to be established, nobody could be saved.

If we needed Israel's signature in order for the covenant to be validated, we would not be able to experience the promise of salvation and new life until Israel first "agreed" to a different covenant. Israelites had their opportunity with the first covenant and they failed. It was time for God to take over and right the wrong for all of humanity. Our inheritance came by the covenant of promise, not the covenant of law (see Galatians 3:14-18).

For those who are of the persuasion the Old was still in place until the temple was destroyed in 70 A.D., it isn't worth debating, because either way, it came to an end. As for those who still think these covenants are to be combined in some fashion, there simply can't be two separate and very different covenants in place at the same time. Jesus came to take away the first covenant in order to establish the second (see Hebrews 10:9). The first covenant had to be completely nullified and wiped out in order for the new one to begin. Therefore, it was made obsolete.

You'll find many in the ministry today who get nervous about discussing the covenants in the context of two separate arrangements, and they are unwilling to concede that the Old Covenant became obsolete when it was put aside and replaced with a new one. Yet we see where this is plainly written in the seventh and eighth chapters of Hebrews. In the mind of God, it was over after the sacrifice of Jesus. However, there were many

Jewish people who came to faith in Christ back then, people who did not yet understand that the Old had been wiped out, and they would still abide by much of it, including animal sacrifices. They would also continue to meet on the weekly Sabbath and read portions of the law of Moses and the prophets, with very limited or no understanding of the finished work of Christ. So in that sense, it was "becoming" obsolete, which is why the writer of Hebrews is taking pretty much the entire book to explain all of this to his Jewish brethren.

As we look back over history, it was a relatively small group of theologians that began to establish church doctrine, which would eventually result into a massive amount of denominations. Today we have a wide variety of colleges and seminaries teaching the study of God, but when conclusions are reached based upon a wrong premise, it leads to a trajectory that misses the mark by a greater margin over time. The covenant combo tradition has led the way when it comes to missing the grace and knowledge of the gospel.

When the apostles came around to teach the revelation of the finished work of the cross in Jewish synagogues, the people begged them to stay for another Sabbath, and the entire city showed up to hear more of this powerful message:

> "Let it be known to you therefore, brothers, that through this man forgiveness of sins is proclaimed to you, and by him everyone who believes is freed from everything from which you could not be freed by the law of Moses" (Acts 13:38–39).

The Mosaic law could not bring forgiveness of sins, life, or freedom and was never meant to be mixed with what *could* bring us these blessings. God did not provide us with a "repaired" covenant as though it were an automobile in need of being fixed. The covenant did not need fixing—the people were the problem. But repairing the people isn't what was called for—what they needed was to die and to receive a brand new life. The old vehicle would have to be sent to the scrap yard, as God provided a brand new replacement that would have an everlasting guarantee. The old bus Israel was traveling on brought them to a stop at the cross, where they would be allowed to transfer to an entirely different and brand new, luxurious bus. To be perfectly clear: it's not called the *updated* covenant, it's not the *amended* covenant, or the *revised* covenant—God said this would be a *new covenant.* The word *new* here means fresh and unused (Strong's G2537).

Following the Blind

As a child, I grew up in a great neighborhood with plenty of kids and good friends. We were part of that generation where you could still leave the house early in the morning, come back after dark and nobody worried about you. I remember a time when some of us were hanging out and one of my friends said, "Mike, my uncle says that verse you shared with us isn't in the Bible." Her uncle was in the ministry, and although I still recall the passage, the reference isn't important here. I went and got my Bible and showed our little group where it was with chapter and verse. I looked at them perplexed as I had just submitted proof that I had not made it up. One of the other kids responded and said, "Well, Mike, he *is* a minister."

The point being that people will often believe whatever they are told if they think they can trust the source. I learned early in life that it's hard to show people truth and freedom when they are content with being led by the blind. There are those who will pay lip service to the concept of freedom, but when it is truly and completely proclaimed as a way of life, the powers of both the political and religious establishment will ultimately resist it.

In my years of radio ministry, I had the opportunity to meet some wonderful people who had a sincere love of God, many who felt turned off by organized religion and preferred to stay away. My personal experience in talking with them is that the vast majority felt they were spiritually and emotionally bankrupt, always falling short of what they perceived was the Christian standard, afraid of being labeled as a hypocrite, or wanting to avoid those who really were. This can usually be traced back to the roots of teaching a Christian casserole of mixed covenant Scriptures, one that often lacks the message of God's unconditional love. The all-you-can-eat church buffet is famous for its spiritual mystery meat, a concoction of various victuals that is unidentifiable and inspires a term used in the military known as *the mess.* Most people have no idea what they are being served. A covenant combination will always mix up the people, and unfortunately, this typical approach has brought judgment and misery to many.

Let's remember that the purpose of Scripture is not to provide us with a bunch of different study topics, but has been given to reveal the person of Jesus Christ. Much like "the Word" referring to Jesus, the New Covenant is also contained in the person of Jesus Christ. Check out this prophecy from Isaiah:

> "Thus says the LORD: 'In a time of favor I have answered you; in a day of salvation I have helped you; I will keep you and give you as a covenant to the people, to establish the land, to apportion the desolate heritages' " (Isaiah 49:8).

Right here we see where Jesus is referred to as the (new) covenant in a day that would bring salvation. The context of that chapter continues with the people no longer hungering or thirsting, just as Jesus shared with those during his ministry while a man on earth. So although the New Covenant was made between the Father and the Son, we have entered into it because as believers, we have been brought into Christ, who *is* the Covenant. We find something similar in another prophecy where Jesus would be made "a covenant for the people and a light for the Gentiles" (Isaiah 42:6 NASB). God would replace the previous covenant with something new and better—his Son.

When Did the New Covenant Begin?

Now we're coming to a crucial point regarding covenant confusion. Religion has made the mistake of thinking the New Covenant began with the birth of Jesus, when in reality it occurred with his death.

> "For where a will is involved, the death of the one who made it must be established. For a will takes effect only at death, since it is not in force as long as the one who made it is alive. Therefore not even the first covenant was inaugurated without blood" (Hebrews 9:16–18).

Some translations in the above passage will use the word *testament* or *covenant* in place of the word *will*. Have you ever had someone die and leave something for you in their will? It didn't go into effect until after their death. So it is with the will and testament (or covenant) of Jesus Christ. As with the first covenant, it was initiated with blood.

> "But when the fullness of time had come, God sent forth his Son, born of woman, born under the law, to redeem those who were under the law, so that we might receive adoption as sons" (Galatians 4:4-5).

Store this in your memory bank because it's of huge importance when putting an end to covenant confusion in our minds. After he was born, the parents of Jesus followed all the customs that the law required for their child according to Moses (see Luke 2:25-39). Jesus was *born under the law* so that he might deliver those who were under it. Deliver them from what? From the curse that the law brought. While he was a man on planet earth, the ministry of Jesus occurred under the law of the Old Covenant, and the New Covenant did not begin until after his death.

The Gospel of Righteousness

Many years ago, a pastor and teacher of grace asked a group of us, "What is the gospel to you? What do you think the gospel is?" It made us stop and think. As Christians, the word gospel was commonplace and we knew it meant good news, but just exactly what was the right answer? I dislike it when someone asks what seems like a simple question I should know the answer to, and I come up empty. It's like one of those trick questions being asked during a job interview and you wonder if there really is a correct answer.

So what is the foundation of the gospel? Simply put, in the gospel is a revelation, or revealing of God's righteousness. Not our righteousness, but his, and it came to be revealed in us. Righteousness simply means justice, or justness, and suggests *the approved condition acceptable to God*. It arrived as a gift through the person of Jesus Christ by faith, apart from works, and freed those from the law who were under its impossible demands. This is one of the foundational truths concerning the gospel and it was proclaimed first to the Jews and then to the Gentiles.

> "For I am not ashamed of the gospel, for it is the power of God for salvation to everyone who believes, to the Jew first and also to the Greek. For in it the righteousness of God is revealed from faith for faith, as it is written, 'The righteous shall live by faith' " (Romans 1:16–17).

This vital truth about the gospel and how it differs from the first covenant God made with Israel will allow us to begin to find a place of rest and peace the law could not bring. With this in mind, put on your spiritual seat belt as we take a closer look at the Mosaic law and commandments of the former covenant and compare the differences between them and the good news that is ours.

(3) THE LAW: MISSION IMPOSSIBLE

WHICH WOULD YOU LIKE FIRST, the bad news or the good news? When asked this question, research shows that the overwhelming majority of those on the receiving end will choose to hear the bad news first. We've got a similar situation with our look at the two covenants.

The bad news came first with the law given to Israel, followed by the good news that replaced it with a second covenant. Why was the law of the first covenant bad news for those who were held under it? Primarily, it was weak and useless when providing perfect righteousness or life and therefore set aside (see Hebrews 7:18-19). So why did such a covenant exist in the first place? Why not just start out with the new and better covenant? In order to find the answers to these questions, we'll need to view this from both sides of the cross, before and after.

Knowing the first covenant is not like the second will bring this clear distinction between the two covenants: *The old way depended upon the people to dedicate and commit their lives towards fulfilling the commands. The new way depends upon the One who already fulfilled the commands and has committed his life to us.*

Let's begin to separate these covenants to further open our eyes to the truth of how we're positioned in Christ. Otherwise we'll find ourselves diving into various Scriptures and start thinking that keeping the old law of commands will lead to life. Even within the Psalms, at times we'll find they revolve around prayers and meditations relating to the law and are a reflection of hopelessness written from those who were trapped in that former covenant. At other times they were looking forward to the promise of redemption that would come through the Messiah. Either way, we don't throw away the passage, we simply look at it from the new covenant perspective we have now. Although it was all they had at that time, the law under the first covenant could not bring the promise of salvation they were seeking. Within some of these Old Testament Scriptures, we'll often read where they kept making the same failed promises their fathers made at Mt. Sinai, unsuccessfully striving to observe and keep all of God's statutes from that law. When visiting the forest of the Old Testament, never wander among the trees without taking the compass of Jesus with you.

Throughout the writings of the New Testament, we see a constant comparison of old covenant law to new covenant grace. "For the Law was given through Moses; grace and truth were realized through Jesus Christ" (John 1:17 NASB). Notice the contrast! On the one hand there is the law that came through Moses; on the other hand, grace and truth realized through Jesus Christ.

What Causes Sin to Increase?

For those concerned that excessive grace teaching will lead to an increase in sin, they have missed the dart board completely. What is it that causes sin to increase? You probably didn't catch this in Sunday school class:

> "Now the law came in to increase the trespass, but where sin increased, grace abounded all the more, so that, as sin reigned in death, grace also might reign through righteousness leading to eternal life through Jesus Christ our Lord" (Romans 5:20-21).

Notice how it is the through the law that sin increases, yet grace reigns through righteousness. Wait a minute! Stop the presses! The law and commandments that came through Moses would *increase* sin? It may come as a shock, but that was its purpose. This is another reason why we know it is not the law and commandments from the first covenant written on our hearts today. If this were true, then God would've clashed with himself because the purpose of the old law was meant to increase the trespass and bring a reminder of sins. Yet in the New Covenant, sins were taken away and God remembers them no more.

Recognizing that God did not give the law to Israel to make them worthy and acceptable of eternal life is a vital component on the road to realigning our thinking correctly with the current covenant of Jesus Christ. The law was *not* designed to aid people towards living an improved moral lifestyle, but rather it was given to show them they could not perform up to the required standard it demanded. In other words, it was designed to fail. The Jews did not understand this, and many Christians have also missed the purpose of the Mosaic law.

I remember a time when my two daughters were very young and playing a card game on the floor. The oldest had to go to the bathroom, so the game was put on hold. I heard the door close. A few seconds later, I heard it open again as she came running back out, exclaiming to her younger sister, "Don't look at my cards!" Then she went back to the bathroom.

As I sat across the room reading, I couldn't help but watch with curiosity out of the corner of my eye. I'm sure the thought of looking at her sister's cards as they lay upside down had never even occurred to my daughter *until she was told not to look.* There was no movement at first as she seemed to be thinking it over, trying to determine if the fruit looked good to eat. But then, ever so slowly, her hand began to move as if it were sneaking up on its prey, trying not to be noticed. Slowly but surely, I saw that small, little hand slide over and start to lift one of the cards. I had tried to stay invisible up to this point, but I spoke up and said in a gentle voice, "Hey, what are you doing?" She laid the card down in embarrassment and replied, "I couldn't help it." Hence, the result of the commandment, "Thou shall not look at my cards!"

Married to the Law

In the seventh chapter of Romans, the Jewish people were described as being in a marriage relationship to the law. Divorce was not an option to be free from Professor Law so this is a marriage they were stuck in. As long as the husband (Professor Law) lived, they were going to stay married to each other. That was a bummer for the bride (the Jews) because the law wasn't going to die; after all it had never done anything to deserve death. Of course the law wasn't the problem—the *people* were the problem. Professor Law was holy, just, and good, but was very demanding, never satisfied, and wasn't going to leave. So how did God resolve this difficult and seemingly impossible marriage situation? Since the law wasn't going to die, Paul explains that the people themselves were killed and made to die. How? *By God placing them in the body of Christ at the cross.* Having died to what they had been held by (the law), the people became free to marry another (Christ), and enter into a new and different covenant.

> "Or do you not know, brothers—for I am speaking to those who know the law—that the law is binding on a person only as long as he lives? For a married woman is bound by law to her husband while he lives, but if her husband dies she is released from the law of marriage. Accordingly, she will be called an adulteress if she lives with another man while her husband is alive. But if her husband dies, she is free from that law, and if she marries another man she is not an adulteress. *Likewise, my brothers, you also have died to the law through the body of Christ*, so that you may belong to another, to him who has been raised from the dead, in order that we may bear fruit for God" (Romans 7:1-4). *Italics added.*

I've heard sermons from that passage that would put the entire focus on marriage and divorce between couples today, but that wasn't Paul's purpose at all. He was speaking to people "who knew the law" and used marriage as an illustration to explain the former relationship the Israelites had to that Mosaic law. The people were released from the marriage to Professor Law because they were made to die through the body of Christ.

You may have seen some very original and creative weddings, but they didn't hold a candle to the production at the marriage covenant between Professor Law and Israel. God officiated the ceremony with Moses as the best man. Who could forget the special effects with the cloud of smoke, loud trumpet, trembling mountain, and the lightning as God spoke through the thunder! When the bride was asked if they promised to do all that Professor Law demanded, they responded, "We do." According to court records, it is well documented they failed to abide by all that the law said to do. It was do or die and a doer could not be found.

Fortunately, Jesus came along and a promise was made by the groom to his bride through a new marriage covenant where he would unconditionally love without demand and would never leave. This time it was the groom who stretched out his arms and said, "I do."

Sinful Passions

Have you ever wondered about the root cause of what actually inflames sinful passions? It's *not* an abundance of grace as some might have you think, and it's probably not what most would assume. Paul gets *passage progressive* as he continues to reveal the problem with being in a relationship to Professor Law:

> "For while we were living in the flesh, our sinful passions, aroused by the law, were at work in our members to bear fruit for death. But now we are released from the law, having died to that which held us captive, so that we serve in the new way of the Spirit and not in the old way of the written code" (Romans 7:5-6).

There you have it—sinful passions (or sufferings) aroused by the law of commandments. Religion has wrongly assumed that the law was given to squelch the desire to sin, but the opposite is true. For those today who attempt to try to live by some form of the Mosaic law in order to attain righteousness or even maintain acceptable behavior, it is not going to result in a success story. Christians have been on a works treadmill for centuries by mistakenly trying to abide in the works of that law, or a modernized version of it. Since the law was against us, the result was bearing fruit for *death* instead of fruit for God. But Paul's good news for his Jewish friends who had been bound to the law is they were now released or freed from it. To some extent, this can also apply for the believers of today who have been bound by various forms of legalism. Paul keeps right on going:

"What then shall we say? That the law is sin? By no means! Yet if it had not been for the law, I would not have known sin. For I would not have known what it is to covet if the law had not said, 'You shall not covet.' But sin, seizing an opportunity through the commandment, produced in me all kinds of covetousness. For apart from the law, sin lies dead. I was once alive apart from the law, but when the commandment came, sin came alive and I died" (Romans 7:7-9).

The commandment brought death and charged sin to one's account, and in Paul's case, it caused coveting of every kind. The law itself was not sin, but because it was opposed to us, it produced sin in us. So while many Christians will assume the law reduces sin and brings life, Paul discovered quite the opposite and makes what may be considered a startling statement: "The very commandment that promised life proved to be death to me" (Romans 7:10). I can only imagine the countless accusations of heresy Paul endured from the traditionalists of his day after making statements such as that.

The apostle went on to say the law was holy, righteous, and good. This was the problem for those who were under it. In fact, it was *so* good, we could call it *demand and supply*, because the law demanded perfection and humans were unable to supply it. The law was also powerless to provide people with the righteous perfection that was needed.

"And you, who were dead in your trespasses and the uncircumcision of your flesh, God made alive together with him, having forgiven us all our trespasses, by canceling the record of debt that stood against us with its legal demands. This he set aside, nailing it to the cross" (Colossians 2:13-15).

The commandments contained within the law were contrary and against those who were under it, and they brought a certificate of debt that now has been removed by being nailed to the cross. *We died with Christ and we were made alive by being raised with him, debt free and forgiven.*

"But now the righteousness of God has been manifested apart from the law, although the Law and the Prophets bear witness to it—the righteousness of God through faith in Jesus Christ for all who believe. For there is no distinction ..." (Romans 3:21-22).

It was not with the help of the law, but *apart from the law* that the righteousness of God was manifested and could be received through faith in Jesus Christ, and "no distinction" simply means it was for both Jews and Gentiles.

"The sting of death is sin, and the power of sin is the law. But thanks be to God, who gives us the victory through our Lord Jesus Christ" (1 Corinthians 15:56-57).

This is yet another passage revealing the law problem for people who would endeavor to keep it—the power, or strength of sin is the law. But God has given us the victory, not by our obedience to the law, but by Jesus Christ and trusting in *his* obedience.

The Unsuccessful Pursuit

Something I find pretty wild is how the Jewish people under the law were not familiar with the righteousness of God. Imagine all the effort of trying to follow hundreds of commands—the constant rule-keeping that would consume your life each and every day—and yet the Jews knew nothing about the righteousness of God. Why? Paul asked the same thing and then answered his own question:

"What shall we say, then? That Gentiles who did not pursue righteousness have attained it, that is, a righteousness that is by faith; but that Israel who pursued a law that would lead to righteousness did not succeed in reaching that law. Why? Because they did not pursue it by faith, but as if it were based on works. They have stumbled over the stumbling stone" (Romans 9:30-32).

I'm going to take a quick timeout for an important clarification: Christians will often assume when Jesus or others speak of *Gentiles*, they are referring to unbelieving, ungodly heathens. While that may be how they were viewed from a Jewish perspective, a Gentile is basically anyone outside of the Jewish race, a foreigner who belongs to another tribe, nation or culture. Obviously, this includes almost all of us. It was considered unlawful for a Jew to even associate or visit with Gentiles from other nations since they were considered unclean (see Acts 10:28). This is why we see the surprise of the Samaritan woman when Jesus asked her for a drink at the well, found in the fourth chapter of John. Thankfully, the gospel and the cross would change all of this.

We should develop the awareness that Gentiles were not included in the first covenant and were never under the law, not before the cross and certainly not after. Yet we attained righteousness by the gift of faith in the finished work of Christ. On the other hand, Israelites spent all of their lives trying to follow a list of over six-hundred laws, commands, and demands they could never live up to, and fell short of attaining righteousness. Ignorance was unknowingly on display when they made this declaration in the era of Moses:

> "And the LORD commanded us to do all these statutes, to fear the LORD our God, for our good always, that he might preserve us alive, as we are this day. And it will be righteousness for us, if we are careful to do all this commandment before the LORD our God, as he has commanded us" (Deuteronomy 6:24-25).

The Israelites had a zeal for God, but they were ignorant on the subject of *his* righteousness. They were too busy working inside of a covenant where they previously declared they would trust in their own ability and became failed keepers of their own promise.

> "For I bear them witness that they have a zeal for God, but not according to knowledge. For, being ignorant of the righteousness of God, and seeking to establish their own, they did not submit to God's righteousness. For Christ is the end of the law for

righteousness to everyone who believes" (Romans 10:2-4).

While attempting to establish their own righteousness through the works of the law, the Jewish people did not subject themselves to his righteousness. It was self-righteousness compared to God's righteousness, and it's vital that we know the difference. It is also crucial that we believers know where the old law ends, and that is with Christ.

The Purpose of the Law

After Paul departed from his visit to the Galatians, others showed up to teach that Gentiles needed Christ, *plus* certain aspects of the law such as circumcision, among other things. Paul's frustration was evident throughout his epistle, and he really bears down in the third chapter of Galatians:

> "O foolish Galatians! Who has bewitched you? It was before your eyes that Jesus Christ was publicly portrayed as crucified. Let me ask you only this: Did you receive the Spirit by works of the law or by hearing with faith? Are you so foolish? Having begun by the Spirit, are you now being perfected by the flesh?" (Galatians 3:1-3).

That was a real humdinger from Paul. Why? In case you skimmed past it, Paul just told the Galatians that their pursuit of works through the law was the equivalent of chasing after the flesh. The problem with trying to keep the old law was that it brought a curse, requiring all of it to be kept perfectly. *We should stop trying to perfect the flesh; God meant for us to abide in a higher form of life.* Paul goes on to share the good news with his friends that they are now righteous by faith in Christ and that the law is not of faith.

> "For all who rely on works of the law are under a curse; for it is written, 'Cursed be everyone who does not abide by all things written in the Book of the Law, and do them.' Now it is evident that no one is justified before God by the law, for 'The righteous shall live by faith.' But the law is not of faith, rather 'The one who does them shall live by them' " (Galatians 3:10-12).

Paul went on to say Christ has brought redemption from the curse of the law by becoming a curse for us, so that the blessing of Abraham might come upon the Gentiles, and we might receive the promised Spirit through faith. So why was the law given? Once again Paul beat us to the punch by answering that same question, explaining it was added because of transgressions until the seed (Christ) would come to whom the promise had been made (see Galatians 3:19-20). Then he offered this slam-dunk:

> "Is the law then contrary to the promises of God? Certainly not! For if a law had been given that could give life, then righteousness would indeed be by the law" (Galatians 3:21).

KAboom! We recognize the law was not contrary to the promises of God, but it could not impart life. It could produce the *desire* for righteousness, but could not provide it for us. This is why we should not attempt to be in relationship with the works of the law. It wasn't designed to administer oxygen, but rather to overwhelm and smother. You can't live by something that doesn't produce life in you. The entire purpose of the law was to cause the people under it to realize they were cursed due to their inability to abide by *all* things written in it. Therefore, it was meant to lead people to the solution of Jesus Christ and to the promise by faith in him.

> "The Scripture has shut up everyone under sin, so that the promise by faith in Jesus Christ might be given to those who believe. But before faith came, we were kept in custody under the law, being shut up to the faith which was later to be revealed. Therefore the Law has become our tutor to lead us to Christ, so that we may be justified by faith. But now that faith has come, we are no longer under a tutor" (Galatians 3:22-25 NASB).

The word tutor means more than just a teacher. It describes a legal guardian who had charge of the life and morals of the boys from a family until the age of maturity (often a trusted slave or servant). It carries with it the idea of a stern disciplinarian (instead of the father). The Mosaic law is described as a tutor or guardian because it constantly brought a reminder and consciousness of sin. Ultimately, Professor Law was a tutor to point people to Christ and belief in him, but now that faith has come, the tutor (law) is no longer necessary. What a tremendous burden to have been lifted for those who had been under it and were now free from the heavy weight that it brought.

Teachers of the Law

Confusion between the two covenants has left many in the ministry with the apparent desire to be teachers of the law, while hanging the heavy burden that it brings around the necks of believers. Please understand that the Mosaic law had a purpose, but it was not meant for the righteous believer in Christ.

> "For some men, straying from these things, have turned aside to fruitless discussion, wanting to be teachers of the Law, even though they do not understand either what they are saying or the matters about which they make confident assertions. But we know that the Law is good, if one uses it lawfully, realizing the fact that law is not made for a righteous person, but for those who are lawless and rebellious, for the ungodly and sinners" (1 Timothy 1:6–9 NASB).

Teaching the law from the Old Covenant as a way to attain or experience life will always result in fruitless discussion or meaningless conversation. It was *never* meant for the righteous believers in Christ. You are now identified as righteous, apart from works.

Let me clarify that references being made to the Mosaic law are not to be confused with the laws of the land in our world today. Obviously, governing authorities have laws in place for people to follow within a society. However, there can be some parallels, as many laws in general have a way of being interpreted differently. Even some of the most brilliant legal minds are often in disagreement as to what a law actually means. This can be found in courts from the law of the land, or by the scribes and Pharisees with the Jewish laws, which would evolve based upon interpretation. Any kind of law in general is meant for those who rebel against what is considered good. In the state where I live, there are hundreds and thousands of laws on the books, but I have no idea what the majority of them are, and I've never gone to the court house to look them up. Just because I'm not exerting effort to keep them doesn't mean I'm breaking them. In fact, I have plenty of friends and family who haven't broken any of these state laws in years, nor have they been trying to keep them. This is the result of them having died and no longer being connected with the laws of this world. Likewise, when it comes to the law from the Old Covenant, we are dead to it so that we might live to God (see Galatians 2:19).

It's a funny thing ... I've never had a police officer pull me over while driving to tell me what a great job I was doing of obeying all the traffic laws. Law doesn't toot a horn whenever we do something right. It's there to point the finger at wrongdoing which is followed by the consequences, and often leads to a sense of despair, failure, and guilt that may result in punishment. While law can attempt to discourage bad behavior, it has no power to stop it, and it's unable to produce within us what grace is able to do—living godly lives and desiring to do what is right, from the heart. Thankfully, the law isn't our tutor for us who are in Christ.

An Expression of God's Character?

You may have heard it taught that the law is an expression of God's character. This can be found in almost every corner of Christianity as well as pseudo-Christian religions. One can begin to believe or assume popular phrases like this are actually quoted in the Bible. Sound bites such as these will make sense at first. Covenant clashers will display a vast variety of verses on the vanity while attempting to connect dots by comparing the law with how God himself is described. As Paul stated about those desiring to be teachers of the law, they often don't understand what they are talking about.

This may be one of those cases where we are arriving at the wrong answer because the right question isn't being asked. Are we absolutely certain the law is an expression of God's character? For example, we know the law states not to steal, cheat, lie or gossip and to love our neighbors as ourselves. Within *the very same law* and often within the same Bible chapter we find instructions not to shave the sides of your face, avoid tattoos, and don't eat fruit from a new tree until the fifth year. Of course, there is plenty more such as not eating pork, avoiding seafood that does not have fins and scales, not wearing a mixture of wool and linen and hundreds of other laws that are now dismissed and ignored. Yet again and again, we find where God repeatedly admonished Israel: "And you shall observe all my statutes and all my rules, and do them" (Leviticus 19:37). All in all, when God says all, he means all. The inconsistencies found in the corporate church world begin to loom very large as we see the *entire* law for what it was meant to be.

If the law is truly an expression of God's character, did God change when he told Peter in the tenth chapter of Acts that it's acceptable to eat the previously unclean animals, birds and reptiles? Did God's character go through a transformation when he told Peter it was okay to associate with the (previously) unclean Gentiles? God clearly declares he does not change and Jesus Christ is the same yesterday, today and forever. What *did* change is the law (see Hebrews 7:12). The Old Covenant was taken away and an entirely new and different covenant was established with Israel, which became a first covenant for us who are Gentiles. The law was just a *shadow* of what was to come, but the *substance* (or body) is Christ:

> "Therefore let no one pass judgment on you in questions of food and drink, or with regard to a festival or a new moon or a Sabbath. These are a shadow of the things to come, but the substance belongs to Christ" (Colossians 2:16–17).

It's time to stop and ask ourselves a relevant question: Why would we attempt to embrace a shadow when we can wrap our arms around the real deal, meaning Jesus Christ? Don't confuse God with the law. Jesus did *not* say, "The law and God are one." He said, "I and the Father are one." *It was Jesus (grace) who was manifested as an expression of God's character* (see John 5:19). Although the law was a reflection of God's perfection, it could not help us to meet the requirement of being made perfect, nor could it provide life or righteousness. Only God could do that and he substantiated it at the cross of Christ.

Establish the Law?

Covenant clashers may agree that Jesus fulfilled the law, but they'll argue we are to *establish* the law by our behavior and adherence to its commands. When it comes to this talk of establishing the law, people will apply what they think should be practiced, without realizing the magnitude of its demands. They get this idea of establishing the law from the last verse of the third chapter in Romans. However, read carefully what Paul stated leading up to it, and more importantly, keep reading into the next chapter as he expounds further. First examine what Paul says leading up to this verse about establishing the law:

> "Then what becomes of our boasting? It is excluded. By what kind of law? By a law of works? No, but by the law of faith. For we hold that one is justified by faith apart from works of the law" (Romans 3:27-28).

Paul begins to illustrate the meaning of righteousness by the law of faith, as opposed to the futile attempt of attaining it through the works of the Mosaic law. He continues by using the example of Jews, Gentiles, and Abraham:

> "Or is God the God of Jews only? Isn't he the God of Gentiles also? Yes, of Gentiles also, since indeed there is one God who will justify the circumcised by faith, and the uncircumcised through faith. Do we then nullify the law through faith? May it never be! No, we establish the law" (Romans 3:29-31 WEB).

If you stare at the tree of verse 31 long enough, you'll miss the forest of context surrounding it. We don't establish the law by trying to keep it; rather we establish the law by pointing people to the opposite—faith in Jesus Christ. Paul is sending out a bulletin that teaching and proclaiming faith apart from works doesn't nullify the law, but rather this proclamation of faith and grace *establishes* the law. In other words, the *law of faith* establishes what the *law of works* was designed to do, which would be to bring a guilty verdict and lead people to Christ. This "righteousness by faith" had now been made available to the circumcised (Jews) and the uncircumcised (Gentiles). You can see this if you keep reading in the fourth chapter of Romans, as Paul continues this theme, but I'll try to hit a contextual climax for you with this:

> "For the promise to Abraham or to his descendants that he would be heir of the world was not through the Law, but through the righteousness of faith. For if those who are of the Law are heirs, faith is made void and the promise is nullified ..." (Romans 4:13-14 NASB).

Did you catch that? Mixing old covenant law with new covenant grace causes faith to be made void and nullifies the promise. Paul continues for the rest of the chapter and beyond to further reveal this gift of righteousness apart from the law. Religion has taught the covenants as though they were two ships that are in sync, but this mixture becomes more like a sinking ship that leaves people in doubt and fending for themselves while being driven and tossed by the wind and the waves. *We don't establish the law by anything we do, so let's get our minds off of our feeble attempt to try to establish anything outside of the gift of faith and righteousness of the gospel.* In fact, it is the God of grace who established *us*:

> "The God of all grace, who has called you to his eternal glory in Christ, will himself restore, confirm, strengthen, and establish you" (1 Peter 5:10).

If Christian believers put any value in keeping commandments and obeying regulations as a basis for acceptance, they have nullified the grace of God and implied that the sacrifice of Jesus was unnecessary:

> "I do not nullify the grace of God, for if righteousness comes through the Law, then Christ died needlessly" (Galatians 2:21 NASB).

As we begin to see the context of Jews, Gentiles, and the two covenants, a door of freedom and grace begins to open our minds to the incredible message of the gospel and will put the focus back where it belongs—on the person of Jesus Christ.

(4) WRITTEN IN STONE: THE MINISTRY OF DEATH

TO GAIN MORE PERSPECTIVE of the bigger picture, let's step back to the beginning of humanity on planet earth and observe the results of the first commandment that was given. It wasn't a piece of good-looking fruit that lured Adam and Eve; the real target with the temptation was to challenge their identity. Essentially, the serpent said, "*Do this,*" and then they would become like the Most High. They lost sight of the truth that they were already like God, created in his image. It is common for us to assume they were trying to rebel against God and pursue sin, or had some type of evil motive. But the temptation was centered on the desire to be more like God, and they chose to take measures into their own hands. The result was becoming like God in a way that God never desired ... knowing good and evil.

During his forty days in the wilderness, Jesus endured temptation in the same way as Adam, in that he was challenged on the basis of identity. The devil came at him with something like this: "If you are the Son of God, do something to prove it; turn these stones into bread!" I think the argument could be made that turning stones into bread might be considered a good thing, but doing *anything* to prove who you are as a child of God is simply the result of eating from the wrong tree. You and I will fight this battle of identity our entire lives, but I encourage you not to give in to the temptation of "doing" in order to identify yourself spiritually. Although it may seem like a thin, blurred line that will be difficult for covenant clashers to understand, the source and motivation for living righteously by abiding in Christ is quite different from the effort of abiding by an inconsistent moral code that is often embedded with an ever-changing set of religious rules.

The tree of the knowledge of good and evil represented the morality tree where man would choose to determine right and wrong based on his own standard, instead of trusting in the life of God that had been gifted to them. The result was passing from life into death, and it affected the entire world around them. Where Adam had been created in the image of God, after his own likeness, sin would cause everyone else to be born in the likeness of Adam, after his own image (see Genesis 5:1-3).

Contrary to popular opinion, it's not likely that Adam and Eve had the intention of trying to rebel with the purpose of looking for a good time with sin or to overtake God's throne. Notice the name of the tree, which could provide knowledge of both good *and* evil, not just evil. Consider the possibility that they may have wanted the ability to discern right from wrong and be better equipped to choose good and avoid evil in order to be more like God. We can't be certain whether Adam and Eve were familiar with evil yet, but we know they were deceived into thinking it would make them wise if they ate. This was the only tree in the Garden of Eden that God told Adam to stay away from:

> "And the LORD God commanded the man, saying, 'You may surely eat of every tree of the garden, but of the tree of the knowledge of good and evil you shall not eat, for in the day that you eat of it you shall surely die' " (Genesis 2:16-17).

This reminds me of a scene from the movie, *Forrest Gump*. When Forrest was given the simple rule by Lieutenant Dan not to get himself killed, Forrest became concerned and was hoping he wouldn't let his commander down by dying. Think about it—only one command was given to man: "Thou shall not eat of that tree." One command, yet man failed to keep it. This was the first example of what *thou shall not* would result into, and we can be assured God wasn't caught by surprise. Adam believed the lie that they wouldn't die, and on that day the first couple began to experience the sting of what I think of as the "killer Bs" that would be handed down to future generations, consisting of bawling, bad breath, bathrooms, and bickering.

Much like Adam, it's unfortunate many people with a desire to please God are still eating from that tree today instead of abiding in the Tree of Life (Christ). There was nothing wrong with the tree itself, just as there is nothing wrong with the law, but they both had something in common. The tree of the *knowledge* of good and evil represents the law, and it was ordained to show us humans that we would be unable to find life in the effort of our morality, ethics, or principles, which is just a new twist on an old approach. How do we know this? Through the works of the law, no one is justified, because it is the law that brings about the *knowledge* of sin (see Romans 3:20).

You see, our moral principles are connected to the wrong tree, and they also become relative, based on our human perceptions, personal perspectives, or the surrounding culture. The fruit from the tree of *thou shall not* may look good to the eye, but it is not to be confused with the fruit of the Spirit found in a better covenant where law doesn't get in the way. Although we're told to avoid the "law" tree that bears fruit for death instead of fruit for God, people who lack understanding of the gospel and the finished work of Christ will be drawn to it with good intentions and miserable results.

The purpose of the commands given to Israel was to show the perfect and holy standard of God, and how their attempt at establishing good over evil would fail and be inadequate, resulting in condemnation. This is not to suggest that the choices we make in this life don't matter. It's good to do good, and on many occasions, we're exhorted to do so. "So then, as we have opportunity, let us do good to everyone, and especially to those who are of the household of faith" (Galatians 6:10). Nevertheless, religion has made the mistake of teaching many that the basis of the gospel is all about avoiding evil and performing good works. That message can be found with some variations in almost every lifeless religion. *But the core message of the gospel is about transferring from death to life.*

Although religion has viewed Adam as a rebellious bad guy who was on a power trip, maybe he wasn't so different from us—having the desire to be pleasing to God and becoming more like him. Since Adam was already like God, created in his image and in a state of perfection, he did not have it within himself to desire rebellion. Adam did not have a sinful nature and sin had not yet entered into the picture for him and his wife. The temptation challenged his belief in what God had said to him. Sin occurred when Adam doubted God and made the decision to take action by trying to fix or improve upon something that wasn't broken. He ended up doing the very thing God commanded him to avoid and then tried to place the blame on someone else—a skill people of all ages continue to master to this day.

It will be a significant revelation for those who are able to see the dots connected in the Bible from Adam to Jesus. Some of those dots that were sandwiched between them included significant characters such as Abraham, Moses, kings and their kingdoms, and the Prophets. Eventually, Abraham would become the example for both Jew and Gentile, as he believed God and was credited with righteousness by faith, apart from works. Along the way, Israel chose a different path and erroneously determined they would be able to fix what was broken by trying to keep the law of works. The Psalms and the Prophets largely reflect on the goodness of the law and the frustrating endeavor at trying to keep it, while announcing the forthcoming replacement solution of Christ. From the beginning until now, God has been attempting to send a message to the people of earth—stop trying and instead make the choice to believe.

Breaking Up is Hard to Do

Many in the religious industry will concede it is no longer necessary to follow *all* of the laws of the Old Covenant, but in the land where covenants collide, we'll find where these same people have volunteered for the committee that promotes the idea that various parts of it should still be kept as an essential component of the Christian life. There is a serious flaw to this approach, so let's consider the inconsistencies while seeing what Scripture says regarding the most "popular" of these laws as promoted by organized religion today.

God declared to Israel that nothing shall be added or taken away from the law. As explained in Deuteronomy 12:32, "Everything that I command you, you shall be careful to do. You shall not add to it or take from it." The inability to acquire life and righteousness under this system was a curse because they were required to abide by *all* of it perfectly. Most legalists in the Christian religious realm don't have much trouble shrugging off various aspects of the law with its commands. For example, the dietary laws are easily ignored, as are the sacrificial laws. But when it comes to the moral laws, the flesh craves to cling to those. Although the church today has primarily thrown out much of the package, it is often emphasized that the Ten Commandments are something we should try to live by in order to avoid sin, attain acceptance from God, and produce fruit. Shame on legalistic religion for diminishing the holy law of God with its crafty removal of large, inconvenient chunks "that no longer apply." Since *all* of the commands were contained in the same package together, the law was never meant to be broken-up, but we should be breaking up from *any* relationship with it.

The problem is this—those giving it their best effort to abide by the law and commandments, and are teaching others to do the same, will cherry pick which ones should be followed, while ignoring others within the package. This leads to hypocrisy because these commands were part of a system or package of 613 laws that demanded all of them be kept perfectly. The luxury of thinking that you should try doing your best to keep a small portion of them would be considered unacceptable to God, because it was all or nothing with the law that came in that former covenant. This is why it would be necessary to replace the covenant, not revise it, because nothing could be removed or added.

Here is a little side note—the Ten Commandments literally means the ten *words*. In Hebrew, the word *dabar* appears over 1,400 times but is only translated as commandment or "commandments" several times in the NASB. Dabar is the sum of what is spoken. Nonetheless, for the sake of avoiding confusion, we will stick with the phrase most everyone is familiar with.

Covenant clashers will try to make the case that we're not required to follow all the Jewish laws since the death and resurrection of Christ, but they are adamant there are some leftovers that are still meant to be applied to the modern-day rule book for Christians. For those who believe every attempt should be made to live by the Ten Commandments, did you drive your car on Friday night or Saturday? Take a walk? Prepare a meal or mow the lawn? Under that system, you are disregarding the Sabbath and are a habitual law breaker. We find where a man was once stoned to death for gathering wood on the Sabbath (see Numbers 15:32-36). That's right, he was one of those stick picker-uppers—you know the type. Clashers will say that type of harsh penalty was put away and no longer applies, and I agree. But the reason punishment vanished is because it was the very law itself that came to an end. If this were not true, all the same punishments for breaking *any* old covenant law should still be executed.

Breaking the Sabbath is pretty easy to see outwardly, so most Christians have found ways to justify keeping it off the required list, in spite of its appearance in the "top ten." After all, the Sabbath rules become conspicuously strenuous when we avoid some sort of modernized version and stay in the proper context of the law. Don't feel too badly about it, even the Pharisees wrestled with this one. Okay, but putting the Sabbath aside, you're still trying diligently to keep the rest of the checklist, so henceforth they shall be called the nine commandments.

But wait a minute—if you've ever had anger towards someone, Jesus said you are just as guilty as a murderer. If you've ever looked at another with a wrong lustful thought, then you are identified as an adulterer, and you'll continue to carry that on your record as long as you attempt to operate within the system of those commandments. That takes us down to seven, but you'll still keep doing your best to live by them, right? What about the possibility that you once desired something that didn't belong to you, maybe even within the past week? Have you always and completely loved God with *all* your heart, soul, and strength, and have you *perfectly* fulfilled loving every neighbor as yourself? Oops, I started slipping in some rules that aren't even in the top ten list. See how easy it is for that to happen?

I'm sure you can see where this is going. You'll keep trying, you'll feel guilty, and then continue seeking more forgiveness from God before starting over and trying harder. Wash, rinse, repeat. It's an old covenant approach minus the animal sacrifices, but with the same failed results when it comes to establishing righteousness, justification, and sanctification.

When it comes to legalists, think of them as people with a "legal list" of rugged, religious rules designed to keep you in line, but are unable to completely carry out for themselves. The list is primarily fabricated, fluid, fickle, and fluctuates from one brand of religion to the next. Previously we saw where James gave two examples from the legalist's short list of favorites. Using murder and adultery as examples, he explained the attempt at keeping the law would mean the impossible burden of doing according to *all* that was written in it. If you broke a single rule, you were guilty of breaking all of them. Similar to what a cable TV company offers with a specific package of channels, under Mosaic law you wouldn't get to pick and choose à la carte which rules to keep, although many will try to do this today. The law came as a bundled package, although it provided no savings whatsoever.

Commandments and Condemnation

If we haven't crossed the bridge already, sadly, we're about to enter into territory where few ministers have dared to enter. Paul is about to share some really exciting news about the deliverance from the entire law, including the top ten commandments. First he will offer a short prelude explaining how this new and better covenant isn't related to a written code that kills, placed on stones or with ink, but it is the Holy Spirit bringing life to our hearts:

> "And you show that you are a letter from Christ delivered by us, written not with ink but with the Spirit of the living God, not on tablets of stone but on tablets of human hearts. Such is the confidence that we have through Christ toward God. Not that we are sufficient in ourselves to claim anything as coming from us, but our sufficiency is from God, who has made us sufficient to be ministers of a new covenant, not of the letter but of the Spirit. For the letter kills, but the Spirit gives life" (2 Corinthians 3:3-6).

God has now made us to be competent ministers of a new covenant of the Spirit, not the old covenant writings that came through Moses. The written letter of the law under the former covenant had a purpose—to kill.

It did it then and it will do it today. But the Spirit brings life, and it is *his* life written on our hearts as opposed to the commands written on tablets of stone. Paul continues this explanation with something that almost sounds like an oxymoron—the ministry of death and the ministry of condemnation:

> "Now if the ministry of death, carved in letters on stone, came with such glory that the Israelites could not gaze at Moses' face because of its glory, which was being brought to an end, will not the ministry of the Spirit have even more glory? For if there was glory in the ministry of condemnation, the ministry of righteousness must far exceed it in glory" (2 Corinthians 3:7-9).

When it comes to the hundreds of commands and statutes found in the Mosaic law, which were the only ones originally carved in stone? This is a red alert, and may come as a shock for those who haven't heard this in church, but *Paul specifically just referred to the Ten Commandments as the ministry of death and condemnation.* Yet time and again we'll find church congregations being taught to work on keeping these commandments starting at the youngest age. It is possible to be on the right road while heading the wrong way. As alarming as it was for Paul to call the (ten) commandments the ministry of death, we'll need to slow down even more because there is a sharp curve ahead that is going to steer you in the opposite direction of where you've been heading. This U-turn will put you on a new course, and if you're going too fast, the ditch will be your next destination. For your own protection and the safety of those riding with you, don't skim past what follows:

> "Indeed, in this case, what once had glory has come to have no glory at all, because of the glory that surpasses it. For if what was being brought to an end came with glory, much more will what is permanent have glory" (2 Corinthians 3:10-11).

The ministry of the former commandments under the Old Covenant no longer has glory because they were *brought to an end* and were replaced by a permanent, more glorious and surpassing ministry of the Spirit. These two roads (covenants) did not merge into one highway. Law Lane became nothing more than an exit ramp with a dead end, while Christ Crossway was our entrance onto the Spirit Freeway, and it was built to have no end.

It's time to take a breath and ask ourselves this question: *Why would we want to start teaching people from the earliest age to cling to the ministry of death and condemnation when it is something that has ended—something the Jewish people were redeemed from, and Gentiles were never under?*

Law and grace were never meant to be a corporate merger, which is why Paul contrasted the ministry of death and condemnation to the ministry of righteousness. This isn't chocolate and peanut butter and they don't belong together. Paul went on to say that when the previous covenant is read, there is a veil that lies over the heart, symbolic of the veil Moses put over his face to cover the end of what was fading. He continues with this:

> "But their minds were hardened. For to this day, when they read the old covenant, that same veil remains unlifted, because only through Christ is it taken away. Yes, to this day whenever Moses is read a veil lies over their hearts. But when one turns to the Lord, the veil is removed. Now the Lord is the Spirit, and where the Spirit of the Lord is, there is freedom" (2 Corinthians 3:14-17).

Notice how Paul shows us that the first covenant *and* Moses were synonymous and hardened their minds. What happens when one goes from living under the commands of the Mosaic law and turns to Christ? The veil is taken away. Every week there are scores of people in Christian churches whose hearts are blinded to a better understanding of the good news because of the reading of that former covenant in the wrong context, and it's certainly not limited to just the top ten commandments. There is an alternative to that old way—the Spirit of God who takes away the bondage and brings freedom.

I recall teaching a class at a church when I shared that passage of the Ten Commandments specifically declared as the ministry of death and condemnation. As soon as I said that, the fire alarms kicked on throughout the building, sirens began to blare, and lights were flashing on and off, but curiously I was the only one ordered to evacuate. Okay, okay, maybe I'm exaggerating just a little. Sometimes I wonder if certain church buildings have been installed with grace detectors. Anyway, someone in the class said she had grown up in a relatively legalistic church, and in all the years she had been there, she had never heard this about the ministry of death. I wish I could say she was the exception and not "the rule."

It's probably no coincidence that the various pictures or illustrations we see of the commandments on the tablets look like tombstones; after all, it was the ministry of death. I'm reminded of seeing a beautiful piece of art where the picture showed Moses holding up the commandments with the caption, "The Law by Which Men Live." The gospel within me recognized it was quite the opposite, it was the law that would prove to be death for people. Ironically, this painting just happened to be hanging in a funeral home.

You can find all kinds of in-depth articles and blogs people have written to argue why the Ten Commandments were separate and supposedly not considered part of the first covenant with Israel. They make the effort to persuade us that the commandments are still in effect today as a "universal law" in order to bring accountability and gain life. It's the typical attempt to connect dots that are out of order and it can sound convincing. Yet there can be no doubt as to whether the top ten were part of the former covenant and the rest of the law given to Israel, as they are called the *tablets of the covenant* (see Deuteronomy 4:13 & 9:9). I can picture God saying to Moses, "Take two tablets and call upon me in the *mourning*." Israel had no idea of the spiritual slavery that was to come.

The Commands Brought Bondage

Religious thinking believes we can attain a moral standard acceptable to God, but it's simply another form of self-righteousness that Jesus tried to discourage. It will lead to either hypocrisy or a false sense of separation from God. Paul used the example of Abraham, which occurred long before the law came. Abe decided to take matters into his own hands by having a child with his servant Hagar instead of waiting for the child that was promised by God through Sarah. These women represent the two covenants:

"Tell me, you who desire to be under the law, do you not listen to the law? For it is written that Abraham had two sons, one by a slave woman and one by a free woman. But the son of the slave was born according to the flesh, while the son of the free woman was born through promise. Now this may be interpreted allegorically: these women are two covenants. One is from Mount Sinai, bearing children for slavery; she is Hagar" (Galatians 4:21-24).

I like how Paul addresses the issue—*"Hey, those who want to be under law, don't you get it?"* In reference to the first covenant, Paul stated the commands given on Mt. Sinai brought birth to slavery (or bondage). What commands were given on Sinai? It included those moral laws carved in letters on stone.

"Now you, brothers, like Isaac, are children of promise. But what does the Scripture say? 'Cast out the slave woman and her son, for the son of the slave woman shall not inherit with the son of the free woman.' So, brothers, we are not children of the slave but of the free woman" (Galatians 4:28, 30-31).

Paul just stated we're under one covenant, not the one that gave birth to bondage, but the covenant that brought us into freedom. The reason for this is because the first covenant was cast out, and our inheritance would be through the will and testament of Jesus Christ.

Is this bashing the law? Not at all; in fact, I would submit we grace radicals have more respect for the law than those who are advocating Christians should try to live by it. We recognize why it was given and that you can't throw out certain parts of it while applying what you feel is convenient. We should have a reverence for its perfection and impossible standard, while realizing it points us to the substance of faith in Christ and his finished work, as opposed to focusing on us and our hollow attempt at dead works.

"For freedom Christ has set us free; stand firm therefore, and do not submit again to a yoke of slavery. Look: I, Paul, say to you that if you accept circumcision, Christ will be of no advantage to you. I testify again to every man who accepts circumcision that he is obligated to keep the whole law. You are severed from Christ, you who would be justified by the law; you have fallen away from grace" (Galatians 5:1-4).

There it is again, take your pick. It was either the freedom of grace in Christ, or the obligation to keep the entire law, but it couldn't be both. It didn't matter if it was circumcision, sacrificial laws, dietary laws, or the moral laws given on Mt. Sinai, nobody could ever consistently abide by the commands, which was the entire point of the law. When we hear the term "fallen from grace," it is usually used in the context of people sinning and not holding up their end of the deal with God. The Apostle Paul stated that falling from grace applies to those who want to continue the failed attempt of abiding by the moral code of the law, rather than trusting in the work of Jesus Christ. The temptation of works is not unlike an alcoholic who "falls off the wagon" and goes back to their addiction.

The New and Better Way

Now that you've had a glimpse at the purpose of the law and what it was meant to do, you can begin to see even more how God was not referring to the Mosaic law being written on our hearts, but something new and different. It wouldn't matter if the Old were written on stone, with ink, or on a new heart, for it would still be the letter that kills and the ministry that brings death and condemnation. This is not a matter of life and death, but rather we have a matter of life *or* death in relation to the old and new covenants.

As we consider context in Scripture, it will help us to avoid blending the two covenants. When a quote from the Old Testament is found in the New, it should not automatically be assumed as an application for the Christian life. There are plenty of old covenant references written by new covenant writers because those Scriptures ultimately pointed to Jesus Christ as a new and better way.

Covenant clashers will insist, "All of the Ten Commandments are found in the New Testament." Considering the many references we've uncovered so far about the law given to Israel and the failed results experienced in that former covenant, do we see any exhortation by writers in the New Covenant for you and I to specifically abide by the list of those commandments? I know people will read this into it because we've been under that assumption, but the answer is no. If this were the case, surely someone would have plainly referenced the entire list of those commands of "thou shall not" in at least one or all the epistles. Perhaps we would expect to find something like this—"Remember to follow all of the Ten Commandments given on Sinai, written on stone, except for the Sabbath." We do not find anything even close to it and have already uncovered something quite contrary.

The scriptural references people point to as the old commands are found in a mixed form of alphabet soup as the writers look back at the former covenant. Something as important as keeping the Ten Commandments would not be embedded in some sort of scattered secret code; it would've been clearly listed and described as the ministry of life, not the ministry of death. It would've stated that Christ is the continuation of the law, not the end of the law for righteousness to all who believe. We would have been instructed that the law is meant for the righteous in Christ, but we're told just the opposite. The 613 statutes were listed quite plainly in the books of the law. Certainly we could've expected that new covenant writers also would have clarified which of the 613 laws no longer needed to be followed, but by doing so, they would've been disobeying the very same law by eliminating parts of it, after God said nothing shall be taken from it. There is a reason why we don't find any of this in the epistles of the New Testament, and it's because the people were freed from the demands of the entire *law package.*

A passage that legalists will use to argue what has just been stated comes from the thirteenth chapter of Romans:

> "Owe no one anything, except to love each other, for the one who loves another has fulfilled the law. For the commandments, 'You shall not commit adultery, You shall not murder, You shall not steal, You shall not covet,' and any other commandment, are summed up in this word: 'You shall love your neighbor as yourself.'

61

Love does no wrong to a neighbor; therefore love is the fulfilling of the law" (Romans 13:8–10).

The exhortation here is that there is a better way than any of the commandments. It's love! God demonstrated his love by Christ dying for us. Jesus fulfilled the law upon this foundation of perfect love. This is why the entire law hinged on loving God and loving others. Although Paul just mentioned four of the top ten, he also said if there is *any other* commandment. This is a reference to all 613 commands found within the law package, and one of the greatest isn't even listed in the Ten Commandments: "Love your neighbor as yourself." So whether it is the "ten words" or any other command, it is summed up in "this" word: Loving your neighbor as yourself.

Leading up to this, Paul spent the majority of the book of Romans showing how Christ brought freedom from the entire law. Paul said apart from the law, sin is dead. Even though he didn't want to covet, the command to avoid it caused him to covet more, not less. So in order to be freed from this dilemma, we all needed to be delivered or made free from *thou shall not*. It makes no sense that Paul would tell people they were released from something and then turn around and tell them to try to live by it.

Certainly there are exhortations in Scripture by the apostles in regards to lifestyle and behavior. They would often encourage people to live from the identity they have in Christ and to do what is right. As the saying goes, rules are meant to be broken. However, true love never does wrong to a neighbor. Love doesn't murder, steal, or covet. It's the right thing to obey your parents, to tell the truth and walk in this love, yet the source for the manifestations of these things is not going to be found in the commands of Moses' rule book or anywhere else. This kind of love is from the source of God himself, by his Spirit, and by grace and truth found in the life of Christ within our new heart as a believer. Whereas the law resulted in the increase of sin, the ministry of his Spirit within us inspires the doing of good and bearing his fruit effortlessly, apart from the demands of the law. When it comes to instruction and exhortation, one way to diagnose if it is law or grace is to recognize whether it's a command with a condition. The old command was almost always attached to a condition, but new covenant directions have no conditions attached.

The Law of the Spirit of Life

The new law of the Spirit of Life brought freedom from the old law of sin, death, and condemnation. This is because we're not under the first covenant with the commandments that ministered condemnation. The ministry that condemned has been brought to an end.

> "There is therefore now no condemnation for those who are in Christ Jesus. For the law of the Spirit of life has set you free in Christ Jesus from the law of sin and death. For God has done what the law, weakened by the flesh, could not do. By sending his own Son in the likeness of sinful flesh and for sin, he condemned sin in the flesh, in order that the righteous requirement of the law might be fulfilled in us, who walk not according to the flesh but according to the Spirit" (Romans 8:1–4).

We just saw the righteous requirement of the law being fulfilled in us. How? By God sending his Son, and Jesus fulfilling the law on our behalf! *God did* what the law could not do (and still can't). God is not trying to fulfill the law through us because this was already done through Jesus Christ. He was fully God, but just as importantly, he was fully man and met the demands of the law perfectly, without sin. Where the law brought condemnation because of sin, *Jesus condemned sin with the offering of his blood.* While the majority of church goers may have been told there is no condemnation in Christ, in the same breath they are taught to live by the very same ministry that brings condemnation, with little or no concept of what was fully accomplished at the cross. *Jesus is our source, our purpose, and our destination, not the commandment.*

Since the law was never intended to be broken-up and distributed in small bites, we should also understand there was not meant to be a different set of laws to be applied to Gentiles (see Colossians 3:9–11). The leaders from the early church in Jerusalem were in disagreement with Paul and other apostles in regards to the law and whether Gentiles should be ordered to keep it. But eventually, even these Jewish believers who were advocates of the law—many of whom were former Pharisees and were yet unaware of their freedom from this bondage—decided *not* to instruct Gentiles to follow the Ten Commandments or other aspects of the law, with the exception of four things:

> "Therefore my judgment is that we should not trouble those of the Gentiles who turn to God, but should write to them to abstain from the things polluted by idols, and from sexual immorality, and from what has been strangled, and from blood" (see Acts 15:19–20).

These four items that they extracted from the law is not instruction from God but was an *opinion* from the James gang in writing for the Gentiles (it is "*my*" judgment"). It is historically accurate but it was not meant to be a commandment from God for all future generations. James had not yet arrived at a place where he felt freedom could stand alone without adding *something* from the ministry of bondage. It appears he chose a few things that may have been considered as more serious parts of the law from their Jewish perspective. Thus began the slippery slope of picking and choosing which laws and commands people think should be esteemed or eliminated.

The grace gang agreed to the terms, after all, they negotiated over 600 laws down to just four. Yet later we discover that Paul and Peter received revelation about those issues such as unclean food and that which had been sacrificed to idols. They would come to the revelation that even these no longer applied to any believer in Jesus Christ. Paul did acknowledge eating meat that had been sacrificed to idols may cause others to stumble who are weak in faith. This is because they were still clinging to some of the old law and he encouraged the free people to be sensitive to those who might struggle with something like that.

In summary, the only way to be freed from the curse of the law was to be delivered from all of it, not portions of it. The law and commandments given to Israel that came through Moses was not a demonstration of God's love, because it brought wrath, death and condemnation. The unconditional love of God was demonstrated to us by the death of Jesus Christ and this love has been poured into our hearts through the new ministry of the Holy Spirit who has been given to us (see Romans 5:5-8). If the system of relating to God through religious rules sounds like a familiar burden in your own life, you've been exposed to the "ol' covenant combo." We have a new guarantee in Christ and it is far better.

PART 2: COVENANTS COLLIDE

It doesn't harmonize with the gospel to suggest that Jesus came with a revised set of regulations for future believers, designed to be harder and more challenging than the existing commands that nobody had ever kept. It's called good news for a reason.

Part 2 Overview:

A. The purpose of the ministry of Jesus under the Mosaic law.
B. Jesus points to something better than the works of the law—the gift of God's righteousness.
C. The invitation for Gentiles to enter into life.

(5) THE NEW TESTAMENT DIVIDING LINE

T HE VAST MAJORITY OF PEOPLE who are considered Gentiles have mistakenly thought, as I once did, that they were included in the first covenant that God made with Israel. At the very least, many will conclude that Gentiles were allowed into some sort of amended agreement where God merged the "new and improved" covenant into the existing old one, as if it were just a better version of laundry detergent. Nothing could be further from the truth. Some of the confusion stems from taking certain things Jesus said and applying them to the wrong covenant. This is founded upon the false assumption that Jesus was always ministering the good news of the gospel under the New Covenant, and everything he taught was meant to be an application for generations of future Christians.

Certain things Jesus spoke weren't meant to be applied directly to us as believers today. There, I said it. But before you stop reading, let me share my thoughts on why I have come to this conclusion. Scripture has been provided *for* us to gain understanding of God and the good news, but clearly not everything was written *to* us. Once we just *begin* to grasp this concept, the Scriptures can become an exciting adventure where a bigger picture appears before us of what God had in mind all along—a plan that was put forth before the foundation of the world, not only for Israelites, but for all people. Most certainly there were times when what Jesus said can be applied directly to us who would eventually be under the New Covenant.

But there were other occasions where he was not speaking to us personally because he was ministering the law to Israel. However, we can still learn from it and realize his Word always has a purpose, and it was recorded for a reason.

Likewise, the same can be said regarding the writings of Paul. It is often assumed when he uses words such as "you" or "us" or "we" that the reference is always directed to Christians. Yet on certain occasions when Paul referred to "us," he meant *us Jews*. Moreover, at times when he referred to "you," he meant *you Gentiles*. If we carefully examine some of what Jesus said, we'll notice some apparent contradictions when compared to what the Apostle Paul said in his writings. Who was right? Of course they both were. On these occasions where there seemed to be conflicting statements, one was speaking from the perspective of the first covenant before the cross (Jesus), and the other was speaking from the perspective of the second covenant (Paul). Again, we must be mindful of the fact that there is a difference between the two covenants and to whom they apply.

When it comes to the teachings of Jesus, it will be helpful if we can begin recognizing whether he was ministering the law, or if it was good news pointing to the forthcoming New Covenant. When Jesus would minister the old law, his purpose was to guide the Jews to a new and better covenant. In order to clear up covenant confusion and gain greater understanding, we must ask:

1. Who was Jesus speaking to?
2. When did he say it?
3. What was he communicating?

"Jesus said it. I believe it." That makes a good bumper sticker—and allow me to say I believe it too. I believe he *said* it, but the question is, was what he spoke meant for you and me *personally*? When we get away from just looking at tiny little verses and step back to see the same thread being discussed over many chapters, it can bring a whole new understanding we've not seen previously. For example, consider The Sermon on the Mount (SOTM), which is three chapters long. I am constantly hearing individual verses quoted from these passages. I'm not saying that it's necessarily wrong to do this, but Jesus spent these three chapters attempting to illustrate man's inability to attain righteousness based on works. It becomes easy to quote the red letter verses out of context and apply them wherever it's convenient or seems to fit with a certain theology. Most of this occurs from the misguided notion that the sermon is a new teaching meant to be administered to Christians today, and we spend time trying to figure out how to make it relevant.

Those of us who believe in free and unlimited grace have been accused by legalistic covenant clashers of running from the words of Jesus. We who treasure pure grace value everything Jesus said, but prefer to approach it from the perspective of context. We don't shrug off, ignore, or run from the words of Jesus or any Scripture, whether it's from the old or new covenant. I think you'll find it is the legal eagles that tend to be selective about things Jesus said, along with other passages related to the Jewish law and commandments. To be clear, everything Jesus spoke had a purpose and should not be discarded or thrown aside. He is the Way, the Truth, and the only way to Life, and it should never be our intention to disregard any of God's Word. However, we should strive to *consider the context* that surrounds what is written and connect to the message of the bigger picture now revealed through the good news.

What Would Jesus Do?

The question is often asked, "What would Jesus do?" Much of the time we don't even understand what he was saying, let alone what he would do. We arrive at the wrong answers when asking the wrong questions. Contrary to popular belief, it is not our primary goal in this life to work at becoming like Jesus. I know this is hard for many to swallow, because it goes against a lifetime of everything that most of us have been taught. Many churches in our culture that encourage replicating the lifestyle of Jesus would be the first to kick you out the door if you walked in wearing the Jesus clothing line.

Adam ate from the forbidden tree because he thought it would make him more like God (it didn't). Israel pursued the commandments because they thought the law of works would lead to righteousness (it didn't). Today believers are told the goal is to work at becoming more like Jesus through the gradual process of self-improvement and lifestyle choices (you can't). Progressive behavior improvement will not make you more like Jesus, but realizing you're a new creation with a new identity that has *already* made you like him will lead to the fruit of the Spirit flowing through you. *You did not give your life to Jesus, he gave his life to you.* It's not up to you to be working outwardly in a way that mirrors Jesus—he will work his life through you from the inside out. We should stop "trying to live like Jesus" and begin to grasp that we live *in* Jesus.

Our identity in him is not based on *doing* in order to become something. We become like Jesus through birth and inheritance; therefore, in order to experience a life that is transformed, we should look to him and what he accomplished on the cross. Instead of speculating on what Jesus would do in any given situation, we ought to meditate on what Jesus has done. It would benefit us to understand this about the Christian life: We can't do it, so he did it, and that finished it.

The Dedication of the Covenant

Prior to the cross, the blood of Jesus had not yet been spilled, so the New Covenant was not in effect at that time. The following is where we find Jesus specifically referring to this covenant that was now just hours away from its beginning:

> "And he took a cup, and when he had given thanks he gave it to them, saying, 'Drink of it, all of you, for this is my blood of the covenant, which is poured out for many for the forgiveness of sins' " (Matthew 26:27-28).

By dedicating the covenant, Jesus dedicated himself. This is not where the second covenant began, but rather it had to be after his blood was shed and death occurred. We know the cup with the wine was symbolic of his blood. Jesus used that same word shortly thereafter when he went to Gethsemane (Matthew 26:38) and prayed to the Father that if it were possible, to let this *cup* pass before him. The word "cup" can mean a vessel to drink from or be used as a metaphor referring to an experience or appointment, whether good or bad. Either way, we can see the correlation:

the cup represented the blood of his pending suffering.

Reality was setting in for this man who was about to have his body shredded and would literally become sin for all of us by dying an unthinkable, brutal death. He knew the sufferings that the Scripture foretold, and he was already experiencing intense agony as he began to sweat great drops of blood. As a man, Jesus seemed to be asking the Father for another way to do this when he prayed, "if it be possible."

This made the Apollo 13 phrase, "Houston, we've had a problem," look like a ride at the amusement park. It's as if the Father was responding with, "Son, we have a sin problem." Jesus submitted, "not as I will but as you will." There would be no other way to accomplish his mission of dealing with sin, which was to do the will of God with a sacrifice to end all sacrifices. Thankfully for us, the mission would not be aborted.

By the way, this doesn't mean we should always use the same phrase, "God's will be done" whenever we pray. Jesus didn't always do this, but it was appropriate for him to do so in this instance. The entire reason he came was to do the will of his Father, who sent him, and it all came down to this sacrifice.

Sermon Prep

As we get ready to approach the SOTM, imagine that the page in your Bible entitled "The New Testament" was not inserted between the books of Malachi and Matthew. Why? The facts below were mentioned earlier, but the importance of understanding them is crucial and thus bears repeating:

1) Jesus was born of a woman, born under the law to redeem those who were under it.

2) A testament, will, or covenant is not valid until the death of the one who made it.

While all Scripture is given by inspiration of God, this *New Testament* page added by the publishers is not considered Scripture, and there is no evidence or reason to believe it was placed there by other than human hand. Quite often, the page may state something like, *The Will and Testament of our Lord Jesus Christ*. The "will" is of no effect unless the testator has died. To get further inside the head of this Jewish audience, let's remove that particular page from our modern-day mindset. Avoiding covenant confusion will help us to avoid getting confused about the teachings of Jesus.

As a newborn child, Jesus was presented by his parents to carry out every required custom according to the law that came through Moses. He was nameless until the eight days had passed where circumcision and sacrifice would occur. Certainly the birth of Christ was one of the most significant events in the history of the world, but it was just a prelude to something even bigger (the cross and resurrection). When the heavenly host appeared to the shepherds at the time of Christ's birth, one of the greatest announcements in the entire Bible was proclaimed: "Glory to God in the highest, and on earth peace, goodwill toward men!" (Luke 2:14 NKJV).

It's a great thing for people to extend peace and goodwill towards one another, but this world-changing declaration wasn't about peace between ourselves. It was the good news that *God* was extending peace towards *us*. Peace between the God of all creation and humankind has now been declared, thanks to the manifestation of The Prince of Peace.

When it comes to the two covenants, they did not intersect or crisscross for a period of time as if some sort of spiritual eclipse had occurred. The Old was in place until the death of Jesus occurred and the New would likely have been ratified right after the resurrection. Jesus came to proclaim the good news of the kingdom, but the Mosaic law and Old Covenant were still in effect at the time of his ministry. Jesus did not proclaim the law as the way to life because it was unable to give life to us. But he would still use it as a tutor to show people their need in finding life that could only come through him, apart from the law.

We're going from Malachi to Matthew, and now coming to this teacher known as Jesus. Let's go to the Mount where Jesus gives his famous sermon. He is speaking to these Jewish people who are under the guidance of the hypocritical scribes and Pharisees. They think they are justified through their law-keeping, but he is about to burst their spiritual bubble.

Jesus had been performing miracles that resulted in large crowds following him. Imagine you lived back at that time. You've heard of this Jesus, but you really have no idea who the guy is. You might know him as the son of a carpenter who spent most of his life working with his dad. He seemed to come from a normal Jewish family with four brothers plus his sisters. It had been rumored his mom was pregnant with him before marriage, and some of the children of the Pharisees would tease him about it in grammar school (see John 8:41). Lately, he had been seen hanging around the temple and had developed a custom of reading prophetic Scriptures before the people. Some were saying he was an unusual anointed teacher or prophet. There were stories going around about how the baptizer dude proclaimed him to be the One Israel was looking for, but who knew for sure. The talk of a Messiah had been occurring for hundreds of years. Rumors were always rampant.

You are on your way to get the water changed in the camel, stopping off for groceries, and picking up some matzo ball soup from Leaven's Bakery. Yet the crowd at the base of the mountain spurs your curiosity, because it's turning into quite a large gathering. As you approach in an attempt to see the man who is causing such a stir, your curiosity becomes so great that you decide to park your animal in the camel lot and slip through the mass of people to start making your way further up the mountain. Somehow you manage to take the right path to where a smaller but still significant crowd is sitting around a man that has all eyes on him. Although there are too many to count at first glance, it becomes evident these are disciples of Jesus. It's easy to blend in as you settle down not far from where the teacher is speaking.

Based on his reputation, the listeners were anticipating a teaching from Jesus that would be filled with new and exciting material related to the coming Messiah. Yet it wouldn't take them long to figure out he was going to begin this sermon with something they were all too familiar with and had been hearing about for centuries.

As you will soon discover, the SOTM was not a new Christian teaching for the purpose of increasing better behavior, but rather an attempt on the part of Jesus to show the Jewish people of that time what the law of Moses really demanded, and why they needed something different. What is about to be uncovered in this sermon may bring you a much needed change of perspective and a view of the forest previously missed.

(6) THE INSURMOUNTABLE SERMON ON THE MOUNT

WE KNOW ABOUT THE TWELVE DISCIPLES that would also become apostles, the band of brothers so unpolished that the Pharisees might have considered calling them the dirty dozen. But Jesus had other disciples and followers, and it has been speculated there may have been hundreds or even more, although many would eventually break the chain and go their own way.

If you were an investigative reporter looking for answers leading to the truth about the SOTM, you would *not* find any indication that Jesus was speaking to non-Jewish people. Although it has been assumed there were Gentiles in attendance, they certainly weren't the primary component of his audience when giving this sermon. Why? You'll find several instances in the sermon where they were told *not* to be like the Gentiles. It's doubtful Jesus was telling them to stop behaving like themselves. While abiding as a man on the earth, the ministry of Jesus was targeted only at the Jews under the law (see Matthew 15:24). After seeing the crowd of people, he went up the mountain and his disciples came to where he was sitting and he began to teach *them* (see Matthew 5:1-2).

In the beginning of the fifth chapter of Matthew ("The Beatitudes"), Jesus starts by saying how they are blessed because of what would eventually be revealed or manifested. "Blessed are those ... for they shall ..." These blessings applied to the poor in spirit, those who mourn, the meek, those who hunger and thirst, the merciful, the pure in heart, the peacemakers, and the persecuted. The word *beatitudes* is not found in English bibles but it comes from a Latin word meaning happy or blessed.

This is a good spot to take a moment and begin to shift our traditional mindset to an entirely different paradigm when it comes to some of the teachings of Jesus. A *paradigm* can be defined as a structured way of thinking, containing basic *assumptions* generally accepted by members within a community. Don't forget who the audience was here: Jesus is speaking to Jewish people of that day from the perspective of their current state under the Old Covenant. This is critical for us to understand as we go forward.

The assumption that Jesus was addressing all future Christians doesn't add up. For example, the *poor in spirit* would not be addressing righteous believers in Christ to whom God willed to make known the *riches* of his glory. Writings from the apostles reveal repeatedly how we have been enlightened and shown the surpassing riches of his grace in Christ Jesus. Those who are dead in sin would be considered spiritually poor, but not people who have been made alive from the one who is rich in mercy, and has blessed us with every spiritual blessing. Gentiles would become beneficiaries of an inheritance within a new covenant filled with these blessings, but they were not the target audience here.

Due to typical teachings on the beatitudes from the wrong context, once again we've tried to make this all about us. The traditional religious point of view puts the focus on *our* doing and our lifestyle. We need to begin approaching the beatitudes with a new attitude and become aware that it was Jesus who would be the fulfillment of every one of these on the list. It is because of what *Jesus did* that we are now in the kingdom. He has become our comfort, our inheritance, our righteousness and our peace. It is only through him we have obtained mercy and a pure heart that allows us to see God and to be called his children. This is all about *being*, not doing.

In the movie, *Saving Private Ryan*, Captain Miller's last words to Private James Ryan were, "Earn this." He and others had lost their lives so that Ryan could live. It can be interpreted as something like this: "Live in a way that shows you're worthy of the sacrifice." In the context of the beatitudes and the gospel, you can't earn this. Jesus was getting ready to lay down a welcome mat before the Jews as they approached a new door where *unconditional blessings* would be discovered.

We'll begin by focusing on this one particular condition because it is the primary theme for the upcoming sermon: "Blessed are those who hunger and thirst for righteousness, for they shall be satisfied" (Matthew 5:6). They weren't blessed *because* they were hungry and thirsty for righteousness; rather, they would *eventually* be blessed because the hunger and thirst would be satisfied and would no longer linger inside a new and better covenant.

Yet there are so many questions about that one short sentence. How would they be satisfied or filled? What kind of righteousness was Jesus referencing? Was it *right doing* to establish their own righteousness through the law, or was it *right being* as the result of God's righteousness? Here's a spoiler alert—he wasn't talking about trying to establish their own right standing with God through their works and efforts. They had already been trying to do that their entire lifetime under the law and kept falling short. Remember what the book of Romans told us about the Jewish people under the law being ignorant of God's righteousness, while also being obsessed with trying to establish their own righteousness through the works of the law. Jesus is now telling them to hunger and thirst for righteousness, but he isn't defining which type. (He will get around to it a little later in the sermon.) This is the beginning of a teaching moment for the pupils that will last for the next three chapters during the sermon.

The Salt of the Earth

Jesus went on to say to these people that they were the salt of the earth and the light of the world (Matthew 5:13-14). We often apply these things to us as Christians today, but he was speaking to Israel, and his Jewish audience understood the connection between salt and covenant, also known as the *covenant of salt* (see Leviticus 2:13-14; Numbers 18:19; and 2 Chronicles 13:5).

Historians have analyzed the close connection between salt and covenant-making. This would generally occur between men during a sacrificial meal and salt was always present. The Israelites had been instructed that sacrifices should be seasoned with salt as a sign of their covenant with God. Entering into a covenant of salt meant binding oneself to another in utmost loyalty, truthfulness, and friendship, even suffering death, rather than breaking the covenant.

But what happens when the salt has become tasteless? Jesus said, "It is no longer good for anything except to be thrown out." Thrown out? That sounds rather harsh! It should be obvious to us this isn't something to be considered as good news, because it's not the gospel. The dissenters will say, "Hey, but this is called the gospel according to Matthew!" Yes, all four "gospel" books have a happy ending with Jesus finishing the work and rising from the dead, but the ministry of the law that would sometimes occur wasn't good news.

It won't bring peace of mind going through life wondering if you've lost your saltiness. Those listening to Jesus knew this was a covenant discussion directed to Israelites who were under the law, and it was involving a covenant where fault was found with the salt (the people). By God's grace and mercy, it would not be the people being tossed away or thrown out, but it would be the *covenant* that needed to be put aside and done away with. Paul exhorted that our speech be with grace, as though seasoned with salt, and James said something similar. However, there is no reference found in the epistles of the New Testament to us being described or identified in this way, so we should shake the idea that we are "the salt of the earth."

In reference to being the light of the world, the people of Israel had been chosen as a *nation* of light, a city on a hill, but had not discovered the light of Christ. Jesus said a lamp is not placed under a basket but is "put on a stand, and it gives light to all who are in the house" (Matthew 5:15). The *house of Israel* is what should be kept in mind here. The rest of the world were outsiders with no invitation into their covenant. When it came to the chosen nation status and covenant Israel had with the one true God, people from other nations were generally unfamiliar with it and would only be allowed to observe from a far-off distance, something like a lighthouse.

Although Israel was once considered the light in a world filled with darkness, in the new covenant of Christ, it is Jesus who is now the light of the world (see John 8:12). Under our present condition as partakers of God's divine nature, we have become children of light in the Lord (see 1 Thessalonians 5:5; 1 Peter 2:9). We are in *his* light, and it's not the same as

Michael C. Kapler

the Lord's reference to the nation of Israel being the light of the world at that time.

As we stay in the context of the sermon, Jesus proceeds with the law and the prophets. Although this is the first specific mention of the law in the sermon, he isn't changing the subject to a new covenant conversation, but it's a continuation of the old covenant speak, and he will stay on this theme as we go forward. Don't miss this:

> "Do not think that I have come to abolish the Law or the Prophets; I have not come to abolish them but to fulfill them. For truly, I say to you, until heaven and earth pass away, not an iota, not a dot, will pass from the Law until all is accomplished" (Matthew 5:17–18).

Recall from our earlier look at the old covenant commands how Jesus fulfilled (or accomplished) the righteous requirement of that law in us. He provided for us what the law could not. To fulfill means to complete and make full (Strong's G4137). The Mosaic law still serves a purpose—to point people to Jesus, but it is not meant for righteous believers in Christ. We are dead to the law.

> "Therefore whoever relaxes one of the least of these commandments and teaches others to do the same will be called least in the kingdom of heaven, but whoever does them and teaches them will be called great in the kingdom of heaven. For I tell you, unless your righteousness exceeds that of the scribes and Pharisees, you will never enter the kingdom of heaven" (Matthew 5:19–20).

Hold everything! The average Jew in the crowd just gasped, "Huh?" Their mouths must have dropped open in astonishment, but those same mouths would soon be closed. If Jesus didn't have their attention already, he had it now. As we attempt to get into the minds of these Jewish people, they had to be thinking something like this: "Our righteousness needs to exceed that of the scribes and Pharisees? The most scrupulous observers and doctors of the law? The pinnacle and representation of righteousness for all others to try to follow?" The Pharisees searched the Scriptures *religiously* and were supposedly the closest thing to a spiritual GPS that the Jewish people had. Yet Jesus was letting his disciples know they would need a greater righteousness.

Clashers will still argue Jesus stated to do the law and teach it. And yet, I seldom see seminaries instructing pastors how to perform animal sacrifices, not to mention the hundreds of other commands and statutes that are overlooked. Just exactly which commandments do you think Jesus was referencing? You can put away the short list from your church statement because it had to be *all* of the 613 commands from the law package, beginning with the least of them.

Again, Jesus is speaking to people before the cross who were positioned in a different covenant while under that law. Let's not forget that Paul chided those who desired to be teachers of the law, as though it were meant to be applied to the lives of believers who have attained the gift of righteousness in Christ. This leaves us with no other choice but to conclude that Paul and Jesus had conflicting opinions and must have "agreed to disagree." There is another possibility and I submit we should go with this instead—there was a different covenant in effect after the cross and *it wasn't like the first one.*

Jesus' statement about *relaxing* the commandments was a direct shot at the Pharisees, who had convinced themselves and others that they were following the letter of the law. Jesus said "whoever does them" would be called great in the kingdom of heaven. We pointed out earlier from the revelation of Paul's writings that there had never been a "doer" of the law. Suffice it to say that you won't find anyone in the kingdom whose name will be appended with "the great." We needed The Great Physician to write a brand new prescription, something that wouldn't be found written on stone or with ink but on our hearts. The old prescription was outdated and ineffective, useless to the people, and needed to be put to an end. Jesus was about to show his audience that their interpretation of the law fell far short of what it actually demanded, and as another Carpenter once said, he'd only just begun.

Jesus will teach the same law that came through Moses, but he will magnify it with the *unrelaxed* version so the people could see what was *really* required to attain true righteousness by works. We know he is teaching the law, as he reflects back to what they've heard or what is already written. When Jesus said, "You've heard it said; you've heard this; you've heard that," he was referring to portions of the law of Moses these people thought they knew and understood, but then he would go on to reveal the unattainable standard of what the law really meant.

Laying Down the Law

Jesus continues with the sermon and begins to teach the law and what it will take to fulfill it. This is not a new Christian teaching for future believers, and certainly it wasn't some sort of new law to be added to the old. Jesus wasn't changing the rules here, but this is the impression many in the church world have given its people. How do we know he isn't changing the rules? Remember, when it came to the law, God stated that nothing shall be added to it or taken away from it. Surely we don't think these people were being given a revised version of the Mosaic law while including Gentiles who had previously never been under its curse. It wouldn't make sense for Jesus to redeem Israel from the curse of law, only to put them back under it a second time, and then begin mixing it with a new Christian law that would be even more impossible than the first! This would have violated the word that God had spoken.

A change of law was coming after the death of Jesus, but before they could enter into the New Covenant, they would have to realize their inability to abide by the existing one. The true meaning of the law that Jesus was about to interpret for them was even harder and more challenging than "they had heard." This wasn't new content, it was simply the Mosaic law revealed or magnified. Red ink signifies debt, so let's keep rolling further into the red letters.

> "You have heard that it was said to those of old, 'You shall not murder; and whoever murders will be liable to judgment.' But I say to you that everyone who is angry with his brother will be liable to judgment; whoever insults his brother will be liable to the council; and whoever says, 'You fool!' will be liable to the hell of fire"

(Matthew 5:21–22).

All right, okay. So you folks know that murder is bad, but if you have had anger with another, it is equal to the same thing as murder. Certainly anger in the heart has been known to manifest itself into murder, and what Jesus just expressed was the law in its purest form. Next we have the sin of name calling. Have you ever called somebody an insulting name? I would imagine anyone who has ever driven an automobile would be guilty of such a crime. In the original language, the word "insult" here means to accuse one of being *empty headed*. If you are familiar with The Three Stooges, this would be the equivalent of calling somebody a *lame brain* or a *numb skull*. (I assume in the Greek it would be pronounced *nyuk nyuk*.) On top of that, if you called someone a fool, you'd be declared guilty enough for hell in a hand basket. Do we Christians really believe this is the good news gospel Jesus came to proclaim? This so-called gospel would persistently put believers in danger of hell for name calling, while offering total forgiveness to a thief being crucified. The reason these seem so inconsistent and even contrary to each other is because there are two different and separate covenants to consider. The sermon continues:

> "So if you are offering your gift at the altar and there remember that your brother has something against you, leave your gift there before the altar and go. First be reconciled to your brother, and then come and offer your gift" (Matthew 5:23–24).

Notice the terminology used with the *altar*, which describes a Jewish old covenant ceremony where animal sacrifices would have taken place. You would be seeking forgiveness from God, but in order for the sacrifice to be valid, you would need to seek forgiveness or offer forgiveness to another with whom there was a division. This wasn't Gentile lingo for future Christians who might attend the First Church of St. Moses.

> "You have heard that it was said, 'You shall not commit adultery.' But I say to you that everyone who looks at a woman with lustful intent has already committed adultery with her in his

heart" (Matthew 5:27-28).

Again, Jesus was using the law to hammer into these people what it was meant to do—bring guilt and condemnation. Even if you *look* at someone with the wrong intent (lust), you're just as guilty of committing adultery as if you did the physical act. Surely a collective gulp could be heard throughout the people in attendance.

Running From the Words of Jesus

Over the years, we've heard many Christian teachings from various verses in the SOTM as if they are a new application Jesus is giving that should be applied to our lives. But somehow we manage to skip over the stuff about cutting off our limbs and other body parts that have caused us to sin, like these verses in Matthew 5:29-30:

> "If your right eye causes you to sin, tear it out and throw it away. For it is better that you lose one of your members than that your whole body be thrown into hell. And if your right hand causes you to sin, cut it off and throw it away. For it is better that you lose one of your members than that your whole body go into hell."

In the land of the legal, they will claim this is just figurative speech and will cleverly explain it away with what they consider to be some sort of a practical application. And this is what legalism does. It will decide by picking and choosing what should be applied, and it becomes relative based on our opinion or personal perspective. Covenant clashers will attempt to intellectualize how this was meant as an illustrative metaphor or hyperbole, an *exaggeration* to make a spiritual point. If that were true, in context, we should apply that same thought process to the rest of the teaching in the sermon.

Was Jesus serious when he said calling someone a fool puts them in danger of hell? Or maybe he was just exaggerating to get our attention for shock value when he said that "looking" is equal to the act of committing adultery. Legalistic cherry pickers of the Scriptures might reason, "Surely he didn't mean looking was *really* as bad as carrying out the actual act!" If

Jesus did not really mean what he said, who gets to be in charge of deciding when he was serious and when he wasn't? If you don't believe he meant what was stated with all of the above, perhaps this would suggest you should throw away your Jesus-said-it bumper sticker.

Whatever words Jesus spoke should never be ignored or explained away. The entire message with everything he said in this sermon had another purpose entirely. It *all* needs to be applied to the *message* to understand why he was saying the things he said. In this instance, he was attempting to illustrate that the only hope for these Jewish people in avoiding sin and meeting the demands of the law, was to start removing body parts *in order to meet the righteous requirement of that covenant.*

Each person listening was already guilty of breaking every single law within the law, but imagine for a moment that they could get a do-over "beginning now" by trying to do it perfectly. It wouldn't be long before the Greek equivalent of "oops" would manifest with yet another sinful mistake. Following a fresh animal sacrifice, the next words out of their mouth would probably be, "Okay, starting *now!*" It was never going to happen as long as they remained in the image of a fallen Adam while living in a body with disobedient members. Imagine the massive amount of healing for eyes, ears, arms, and legs that would've occurred after the sermon if everyone had followed through with removing parts of the body and throwing them away.

Instead of seeing this passage as purely metaphorical, let's consider the possibility Jesus was using just a bit of sarcastic humor to show the impossibility of trying to keep the law. The true purpose for saying all of these things wasn't to inspire them to cut off body parts, but to help them see the hopelessness of their position under the Mosaic law and show them a better way. As we put away the black highlighter, we'll begin to see the full sermon in the proper context. Jesus meant what he said.

High Hurdles

For the rest of the chapter, the red letters of Jesus just keep pounding away as the growing audience must have felt themselves shrinking inside. "You have heard it said ... You have heard the ancients were told ... *But I say to you...*" With each command Jesus referenced, he made it more and more impossible than what the original appeared to require. Divorce and adultery, false vows, oaths, if you get slapped then turn the other cheek. If they slap that one give them the first cheek to swat. Again, think in terms of The Three Stooges—you suddenly just became Curly, and Moe is allowed to slap you silly.

> "If anyone wants to sue you and take your shirt, let him have your coat also. Whoever forces you to go one mile, go with him two. Give to him who asks of you, and do not turn away from him who wants to borrow from you" (Matthew 5:40-42 NASB).

Never turn anyone away. Have you ever done this? Jesus proceeds to drop a nugget about loving even those who were considered the enemies of Israel, but this was nothing new as we can find such references in the Old Testament, and we'll see later that the entire law and the prophets were centered on this. As the sermon progresses, it's one example after the other of Jesus appearing to raise the bar, with the high jump of works getting higher. In reality, Jesus didn't raise the bar higher than it already was except in the minds of his audience. He simply told these people who were under the law what it actually demanded and required.

> "For if you love those who love you, what reward do you have? Do not even the tax collectors do the same? And if you greet only your brothers, what more are you doing than others? Do not even the Gentiles do the same?" (Matthew 5:46-47).

Even the Gentiles can live up to what you're doing. This was a low blow that must've cut pretty deep. Our modern-day mindset doesn't understand the despising of the lowly, unclean Gentiles. At one point, Jesus even compared them to dogs, and many Jews probably felt his comment was an insult to pooches everywhere. It's another reminder that the target audience here in this sermon is for Israel, not for people outside the Jewish race who had no relationship to the law or that covenant, not then or now.

Are you ready for the last verse in the chapter? "You therefore must be perfect, as your heavenly Father is perfect" (Matthew 5:48).

With the word *therefore*, we know Jesus just summarized his sermon up to this point and it's a doozy of a summary. Do you want to get to heaven by doing it right and meeting the righteous requirement of the law? It will demand more than your best effort; it will call for pure perfection, just like that of God Almighty.

If you had been a listener in the crowd, you probably would have found this to have been a pretty discouraging message up to this point. But then to top it off, Jesus suddenly dumps this perfection requirement on you. Everything Jesus said within the entire sermon was wrapped up in this one sentence of *you must be perfect.* I don't know about you, but I would've been thinking there is no way I could live up to this standard. And that's all Jesus was looking for—someone to stand up and say, "This is impossible! Nobody can do this!" In fact, I can remember a time in my own life as a teenager when I told God I couldn't live up to what I thought were the demands of the Christian life, and it made me want to give up and quit trying. I hadn't realized at the time this was the conclusion and place where he wanted me to arrive.

Something fascinating about the word "perfect" here in Matthew is that the Greek word for it is *teleios,* and it suggests "to be made complete, full grown, lacking nothing necessary." In comparison, when Jesus hung on the cross and said, "It is finished," the word for *finished* has the same basic meaning—"to end, fulfill, pay, and accomplish." While these both originate from the same Greek word, the difference is that *perfect* is an adjective and *finished* is a verb. "You must be perfect" is describing a potential Godlike quality about us and a state of being, whereas "it is finished" tells us the act or the experience of what Jesus did to make it happen. If you're not yet seeing this astonishing connection between our perfection and the finished work of Christ, I hope your heart will relate to it as we go forward. Jesus actively became our perfection by fulfilling the commandment, and he would be the executor of his own will and testament.

Clashers will reason since we are required to be perfect and the law is perfect, we should follow, obey and try to keep the law in order to attain perfection, holiness and sanctification. It makes sense except for one itsy-bitsy, teeny-tiny detail—the law makes nothing perfect (see Hebrews

7:19). Righteousness and perfection can't come to us by *any* law, otherwise Jesus never would have had to die. Notice how those "law-abiding citizens of the kingdom" will never advocate keeping *all* that was written in the law. This approach goes against what the very law itself required and the hypocrisy of it should be exposed in order to proclaim the true gospel message.

"You are perfect for me." This is known to be a popular phrase communicated between romantic couples. Similarly, Jesus is perfect *for* you. If you aren't perfect, you need someone to represent you who is.

> "Now we know that whatever the law says it speaks to those who are under the law, so that every mouth may be stopped, and the whole world may be held accountable to God. For by works of the law no human being will be justified in his sight, since through the law comes knowledge of sin" (Romans 3:19-20).

Paul went on to say that there would be no more boasting regarding the law of works but by a new law of faith (in Christ). The purpose of the SOTM was to minister what the law was always meant to do—bring people to the end of themselves and their works while pointing them to the Messiah and Redeemer.

Jesus came to close every mouth. Their boasting days were over.

(7) THE LORD'S PRAYER

ALTHOUGH WE'RE ABOUT TO ENTER the sixth chapter of Matthew, the same sermon continues on the same Mount, and we should be mindful of how Jesus stays on point. He isn't hopscotching through a myriad of different topics, but continues with the same thread he began with. Pay special attention to how this chapter begins and what Jesus said, because we're about to come to a crossroads, or a fork in the road at the corner of Self-Effort Street and Righteousness Road. I well remember this corner in my own life.

> "Beware of practicing your righteousness before other people in order to be seen by them, for then you will have no reward from your Father who is in heaven. Thus, when you give to the needy, sound no trumpet before you, as the hypocrites do in the synagogues and in the streets, that they may be praised by others. Truly, I say to you, they have received their reward" (Matthew 6:1-2).

Be cautious of practicing *your* righteousness before others. Earlier in the sermon, Jesus told the Jews that their righteousness would need to exceed that of the Pharisees. While opening the door to abiding in God's righteousness, he was slowly beginning to transition their thinking from the hollow attempt of establishing their own righteousness through the law. Some might say that Jesus meant to be careful about their practicing righteousness with the *purpose* of being noticed by others. But that's what self-righteousness does—it instinctively seeks to be noticed, and the only reward it will bring is human recognition for one's good efforts. In other words, you can't attempt to establish *your* righteousness without the inward motive of outwardly being noticed by others. As the prophet Isaiah said, their righteous deeds had become like filthy garments.

The flesh yearns for the applause, approval, and recognition of others. It falsely reinforces confidence in one's own spiritual stature and wrongly convinces the aspiring doer of the law that they have advanced their position with God through their actions. It will always fall short, and because of that, self-righteousness will continue to seek further attempts and opportunities to establish itself. But it can never take root in the rocky soil of its own effort. Jesus had a purpose for this sermon to the Jewish people and that was to point out the futility of thinking they could attain right standing with God by trying to keep the demands of the law. He is methodically revealing the true purpose as to why the law was given along with the Jews' inability to follow it perfectly. Jesus is on a mission to get them off the drug of self-righteousness as he continues:

> "And when you are praying, do not use meaningless repetition as the Gentiles do, for they suppose that they will be heard for their many words. So do not be like them; for your Father knows what you need before you ask Him" (Matthew 6:7-8 NASB).

Wow, has religion ever skipped over that one—avoiding meaningless repetition as the *Gentiles* do. Another translation states not to heap up empty phrases. I can almost hear the religionists of today saying, "Preach it, Jesus! Don't be like those silly Gentiles who are far off and without God in the world!" I'm about to state the obvious, but it's one of those things that often goes unrecognized by Christians—anyone who isn't born of the Jewish race is automatically in the Gentile category. Therefore, Jesus is about to tell the Jewish people positioned under the Mosaic law what *they* should pray for.

Now I'm getting ready to tread on what many will consider to be sacred ground and off limits. They will declare some traditions were never meant to be broken, and may hurl accusations of blasphemy and false teaching, in spite of how little they know about the tradition they wish to defend. This is where many will stake their claim and tell me to keep off their grass by planting a sign that says *No Trespassing!* Speaking of trespassing ...

> "Pray then like this: Our Father in heaven, hallowed be your name. Your kingdom come, your will be done, on earth as it is in heaven. Give us this day our daily bread, and forgive us our debts, as we also have forgiven our debtors. And lead us not into temptation, but deliver us from evil" (Matthew 6:9-13).

We've put this prayer on an island by itself, but it belongs in the context of what Jesus said prior to and after he spoke it. To put it in perspective, this prayer was being offered to *these* people of Israel at *that* time. Jesus just got done saying not to use meaningless repetition when they prayed, repeating the same thing over and over like we Gentiles would do. What is it the church world has done with this prayer? It seems to me Gentiles everywhere have done the very thing that Gentiles did back then, and it's precisely what Jesus said not to do. The prayer gets repeated constantly and we usually sound like monotone robots when we do it, because there is no heartfelt life in memorizing a script when communicating with anyone. It is not a prayer for Gentiles under the New Covenant, and this would've been a no-brainer for the Jews listening because it was clear to them that Jesus was having a covenant conversation of which outsiders had no part.

This example of how to pray would've had meaning for those under the law prior to the cross, but for us who are under a New Covenant, there is no reason to be repeating these phrases that now echo a certain emptiness, because Jesus fulfilled the prayer with his finished work. Regardless of the specific words used by Christians when praying, it is my observation that *we are frequently asking and seeking for what God has already given.*

We call it the Lord's Prayer. It has been said it might be more accurately described as the Disciples Prayer, since it was provided for them to pray. The seventeenth chapter of John would be a better fit for a title of the Lord's Prayer. But with this prayer in mind, remember the context leading up to it, along with what will follow. Jesus is still ministering a message to people under the law, before the suffering of the cross and the victorious resurrection. We need to begin to see the perspective in which he provides his audience with this prayer. Unlike a religious television or radio program of today, Jesus did not take a timeout for a promotional commercial break that just popped up in the middle of his teaching—"And now here's a 'word' from our sponsor *(insert prayer)*. The Lord's Prayer has been made possible by Holy Scroller Ministries. Now back to our regularly scheduled sermon about self-righteousness and the impossible law that requires perfection."

Some will agree this prayer was not necessarily meant to be repeated, but they will suggest it is to be used as a model prayer for us today. I'll respectfully disagree and submit that the Lord's Prayer was no more meant to be a model for us under the New Covenant than plucking out eyes or cutting off limbs was meant to help Israel fulfill the law. Reciting the prayer just seems like the proper religious thing to do because we've assumed Jesus is speaking to us as Christians, but I believe we're getting our covenants mixed up. Be aware that leading up to this, Jesus had just given them a message of hopelessness when he revealed they were required to be perfect in obeying the law and commandments—righteousness was out of their reach. With that in mind, let's break this down in chunks to help reveal the meaning of the prayer and why Jesus told those who were under the old covenant law to pray in this way.

Our Father in Heaven: You may have been taught that Israelites would not have been able to relate to the concept of God as "Father." There are numerous places in the Old Testament that show otherwise. A few examples are found in Deuteronomy 32:6; 1 Chronicles 29:10; and Jeremiah 31:9. The opening line to this prayer wasn't necessarily a new expression for these Jewish people, they recognized Father God in heaven, and that he is holy. However, they would not have understood the mystery of "Christ in you," which would later be revealed when the New Covenant was inaugurated, after the death of Jesus.

For many, heaven seems like a distant planet with infinite space between us and God. The presence of the Father is no longer quarantined or limited to a place called heaven. We now live in the New Covenant where God abides in us and has promised never to leave. If you have the picture in your mind that God's ZIP code is just in heaven, this is a reminder that he also has a new address—in you.

In regards to the Father's name being hallowed or holy, we won't go into detail about the utmost reverence that the Jewish people had for the name of God except to say his name was not "God." However, with the revelation of the New Covenant, it should be pointed out that the name which is above *every* name is Jesus Christ (see Philippians 2:9-11).

In your spare time, look through the sixteenth chapter of John and observe Jesus conversing with his disciples as he nears the end of his time on earth, and looks ahead to the day of the New Covenant. He reveals to them that he would be leaving, and the Spirit of truth would come and guide them into all truth. They were instructed by Jesus to do something different "in that day," and that would be to pray to the Father *in his name*. Jesus did not give such instruction with this prayer during the sermon. It's another clue that it was provided only to people under the first covenant for them to pray before the cross, at a time when Jesus was not the High Priest.

Your Kingdom Come: Despite how often we may hear the phrase, "the kingdom of God," it can be a somewhat mysterious and difficult concept to grasp. I realize what I am about to share will draw people into the thickness of the theological weeds, and you'll hear a lot of different viewpoints about the kingdom, but my perspective is quite simple.

The word *kingdom* in the Greek language is *basileia*, defined as "kingship, sovereignty, authority, rule." With that explanation in mind, it is worth noting some word studies will state it is not to be confused with an actual kingdom, but rather the right or authority to rule over a kingdom, or the realm in which a king rules. A kingdom requires a king and cannot be defined apart from the king, otherwise it's not a kingdom. Therefore, it can be interpreted that the word *kingdom* is not necessarily referring to a kingdom by itself, but is meant to include the ruler of the kingdom (Jesus). Shortly before his death, we find in the eighteenth chapter of John where Jesus told Pilate his kingdom was not of this world. Pilate's instant response: "So you are a King?" He understood you couldn't have one without the other.

When we talk about preaching the kingdom, this can't be done apart from the message of the person of Jesus—the Ruler, Messiah and the King of kings. Here is one example of the Apostle Paul testifying about the kingdom of God to some leaders of the Jews:

> "When they had set a day for Paul, they came to him at his lodging in large numbers; and he was explaining to them by solemnly testifying about the kingdom of God and trying to persuade them concerning Jesus, from both the Law of Moses and from the Prophets, from morning until evening" (Acts 28:23 NASB).

Paul wasn't relaying a message about a future kingdom, but one that has arrived through Jesus Christ as was foretold during the first covenant. He has *already* come and he conquered at the cross.

In Revelation 1:5-6, John recorded that the church has been freed from sins by the blood of Jesus and many translations state he has made us to be a "kingdom and priests." The NKJV translates it that we have been made kings and priests. So we can see the similarities between "king and kingdom." From a scientific perspective, Christ is the *substance* of the kingdom and they can't be separated.

Paul beautifully described the kingdom of God as "righteousness, peace, and joy in the Holy Spirit." Righteousness and the kingdom of God are also inseparable and Jesus will soon be revealing this truth by the end of the sixth chapter of Matthew. This kingdom is not about a government that is of the people, by the people, and for the people. This government will rest upon the shoulders of the Son with a kingdom that will have no end, and it will be upheld in righteousness (see Isaiah 9:6-7). Isaiah also foretold of what would occur when "a king reigns in righteousness" in the 32nd chapter of his book. It has a happy ending.

People today have it in mind they are praying for a future kingdom that will occur at the end of this world. It is often based on the *assumption* Jesus was instructing all forthcoming generations to chant this prayer as a repetitious ritual or use it as a model. I find it difficult to fathom that Jesus was telling everyone who would ever walk the planet from that time forward, to repeatedly pray for something that would never occur in their earthly lifetime. In context, I believe he was referring to something more imminent, meant for those to whom he was speaking.

Interestingly, when Jesus began his ministry he said the kingdom of heaven is at hand. In Matthew 12:28, Jesus said, "But if it is by the Spirit of God that I cast out demons, then the kingdom of God has come upon you." In Luke 17:21 when asked when the kingdom of God would come, Jesus said *it wouldn't come as something to be observed* as if you could say it was here or there, but that "the kingdom of God is in the midst of you." This is a biggie because how does one go about describing the kingdom in terms of it being inside of you? You see, it all centers around Jesus.

Even if you want to view the kingdom of God as some type of realm or domain where people live, exist or abide, guess where we abide in the current covenant? In him! Jesus is the ruler of the territory. Therefore, it's time to take a breath and ask ourselves this question: Under the New Covenant, *why should believers pray for the kingdom to come when it has already arrived with King Jesus who lives within us, and in whom we live, move and exist?* The answer is—we shouldn't. After the cross, we are never instructed to pray for God's kingdom to come in any of the epistles from the apostles. Pause to think about all the emphasis placed on "your kingdom come" and the Lord's prayer today. Surely at some point, at least one of the apostles would've suggested praying in this way! But it's nowhere to be found because as believers "we have *received* a kingdom that cannot be shaken" (see Hebrews 12:28).

Your Will Be Done: Jesus said to pray that God's will would be done on earth as it is in heaven. We often think in terms of God's overall will for many things taking place in the world, but there is something more specific being addressed here, and it has to do with our redemption. In the tenth chapter of Hebrews, we can see how Jesus executed the will of God on the earth through the offering of his body that God had prepared for him.

> "Consequently, when Christ came into the world, he said, 'Sacrifices and offerings you have not desired, but a body have you prepared for me; in burnt offerings and sin offerings you have taken no pleasure.'
>
> "When he said above, 'You have neither desired nor taken pleasure in sacrifices and offerings and burnt offerings and sin offerings' (these are offered according to the law), then he added,

'Behold, I have come to do your will.' He does away with the first [covenant] in order to establish the second. And by that will we have been sanctified through the offering of the body of Jesus Christ once for all" (Hebrews 10:5-6; 8-10). *Brackets added by author.*

Step back now to allow for a better view of the bigger picture of God's will, which was to have Jesus give himself for our sins and to rescue and deliver people from the present evil age (see Galatians 1:4). The Greek word for "will" in the book of Hebrews is the same as what we find in the prayer. God's will *has* been done by having Christ sacrificed, which brought us our perfection, justification, and allowed for the first covenant to be replaced with the second one.

On Earth as it is in Heaven: After Jesus was sacrificed on this earth, he did not go into the replica tabernacle made by humans, which was only a copy and shadow of the real deal:

> "But when Christ appeared as a high priest of the good things that have come, then through the greater and more perfect tent (not made with hands, that is, not of this creation) he entered once for all into the holy places, not by means of the blood of goats and calves but by means of his own blood, thus securing an eternal redemption" (Hebrews 9:11-12).

Jesus went into heaven and into the perfect tabernacle before the presence of God himself, appearing on our behalf with a sacrifice worthy of heaven. It was the better sacrifice that replaced all other insufficient sacrifices.

> "That is why the Tabernacle and everything in it, which were copies of things in heaven, had to be purified by the blood of animals. But the real things in heaven had to be purified with far better sacrifices than the blood of animals" (Hebrews 9:23 NLT).

Notice the plural in the word "sacrifices" referring to the heavenly place. This may seem confusing since Christ offered only one sacrifice. A commonly held view to consider is this: In Leviticus 1-5, Israel was appointed five offerings. They were the burnt, the meal (grain), the peace, the sin, and the guilt offering. In the *one* completed sacrifice of Christ we have a representation or antitype of *all* of them.

> "For Christ did not enter into a holy place made with human hands, which was only a copy of the true one in heaven. He entered into heaven itself to appear now before God on our behalf. And he did not enter heaven to offer himself again and again, like the high priest here on earth who enters the Most Holy Place year after year with the blood of an animal. If that had been necessary, Christ would have had to die again and again, ever since the world began. But now, once for all time, he has appeared at the end of the age to remove sin by his own death as a sacrifice" (Hebrews 9:24-26 NLT).

His sacrifice would not have to be repeated on the earth as it had previously with the Jewish high priests. The earthly priests would be required to leave, and then return to the tabernacle again and again to stand and minister more of the same, never once taking away sins. The will of God performed with this sacrifice on earth would satisfy the requirement in heaven by the everlasting *removal of sin*, to be remembered no more.

Give Us This Day Our Daily Bread: Jesus instructed these people under the Old Covenant to pray for their daily bread. The view from our traditional paradigm will frequently assume people are to pray each day for physical food and similar needs. However, a few verses after the prayer, Jesus told them not to worry about food for the body, so let's identify the daily bread as Jesus himself, because this is what they needed to pray for. As they prayed for God's will to be done, they should be looking for the day of salvation that was yet to arrive. As you may recall, the day of salvation is when Jesus would become a covenant for the people, a passage found in the book of Isaiah that the Apostle Paul also referred to in 2 Corinthians 6:2. We now live in that day.

A paraphrase of what Jesus is saying might be something like this: *"Pray that God's will is accomplished by providing the day of salvation with the bread of life."* Jesus even prayed for this will of the Father to be completed shortly before his arrest in the Garden of Gethsemane, and he was asking some of these same disciples to do the same. At the time of the sermon when Jesus gave his disciples this prayer, God's will had yet to be completed in regards to the work of redemption.

I find it intriguing the only time the Greek word for "daily" is found in scripture is during the Lord's Prayer (Strong's G1967). It basically means something that is necessary and sufficient for each day. Jesus is that source of bread that gives us life and our existence. As Paul wrote in 2 Corinthians 4:16: "So we do not lose heart. Though our outer self is wasting away, our inner self is being renewed day by day." There is no longer the need for us who are in Christ to ask God for the bread of Jesus, since he has *already* given us this gift of his Son.

In the book of John, observe what Jesus said about being the bread that came from heaven, and the parallel with the perspective provided about the Lord's Prayer. He is the bread that came to do God's will:

> "For the bread of God is he who comes down from heaven and gives life to the world." They said to him, 'Sir, give us this bread always.' Jesus said to them, 'I am the bread of life; whoever comes to me shall not hunger, and whoever believes in me shall never thirst' " (John 6:33–35).

Jesus is the bread from heaven, and he is looking ahead to when the day of salvation would be given and those who believe would not hunger or thirst again. Contrast that to when Jesus started the SOTM regarding those who hunger and thirst for righteousness *before* the cross. The passage continues in connecting the bread of life that came from heaven with doing the ultimate will of God:

> "For I have come down from heaven, not to do my own will but the will of him who sent me. And this is the will of him who sent me, that I should lose nothing of all that he has given me, but raise it up on the last day. For this is the will of my Father, that everyone

who looks on the Son and believes in him should have eternal life, and I will raise him up on the last day" (John 6:38-40).

Recall the Lord's introduction of a new covenant at the Last Supper and how bread symbolized his body that would be broken. Bread not only breaks, but it rises when made new. Jesus is the bread of life that was broken but now has risen; you were raised with him, and God isn't going to lose you! In this same chapter of John, Jesus said not to seek the food that perishes. He compared himself to the manna that daily fed the Jews in the wilderness (see Exodus 16:4). What manna was to Israel in a physical sense, Jesus is to us spiritually as supernatural food. Those who ate manna in the wilderness died, but whoever eats of the living bread from heaven will live forever, and we partake of this bread by *believing*. Jesus got specific when he said the bread he would give for the life of the world was his flesh (see John 6:47-51). Instead of asking God for what has already been given, thank him for it!

Forgive Us As We Forgive Others: This prayer for the Jewish people was leading them to seek forgiveness for sins *based on the condition* that they have forgiven others who have sinned against them. After Jesus is done with the description of how to pray, he sums up the prayer with the *law*, by returning to the subject of conditional forgiveness:

> "For if you forgive others their trespasses, your heavenly Father will also forgive you, but if you do not forgive others their trespasses, neither will your Father forgive your trespasses" (Matthew 6:14-15).

Insert another collective gulp here from the disciples. That statement ranks right up there with the challenge of "you shall be perfect." We know the prayer revolved around what Jesus just said because it was echoed right afterwards and started out with the word *for*, looking back on something that was previously stated.

"Forgive us for our sins as we forgive those who sin against us." *This literally means that you would be asking to be forgiven by God in a way that is equal to how you forgive others.* Uh-oh. Was this good news for the hearers?

No! Why? Nobody had ever achieved forgiving others perfectly from within their heart. Before the cross, we find forgiveness was based on the condition that they also forgive others—this was the reality for the Jews in the Old Covenant and Jesus addressed this earlier in the sermon when talking about sacrifices and offerings at the altar. I seriously doubt we want that particular wrecking ball hanging over our heads, waiting to drop on our eternity. Jesus gave them an example of what to pray regarding the kingdom of *righteousness*, and then included the current reality that forgiveness was conditional where they were positioned at that time under the law.

Under that Old Covenant, they were going nowhere fast, and needed the will of God to be done by having their King deliver them from evil and from the hopeless burden of their forgiveness being dependent upon themselves. I repeat, *they were in a hopeless position if their forgiveness depended on forgiving others.* Yet this is what Jesus was ministering—hopelessness and despair through the law. Once God's will would be done and completed, they could be freed from the mess of being required to behave perfectly, selling everything they had, and cutting off limbs to avoid sin.

Should we forgive others today? Absolutely and unconditionally! However, under a better covenant, we don't forgive in order to be forgiven, but *because* we're already forgiven. Looking at it from this side of the cross, Paul put it this way: "Be kind to one another, tender-hearted, forgiving each other, just as God in Christ also has forgiven you" (Ephesians 4:32). It would be difficult for a person to give something to another if they had not yet received, possessed, or experienced it for themselves (everlasting forgiveness). That was the problem under a covenant involving the works of the law.

In the New Covenant, we should not be striving to gain a position of favor with God, because we were gifted with favor and now live out of response from that established position we have in Christ. *If our forgiveness from God is dependent upon us forgiving others, then we're not under faith but back to a system of works that Jesus called impossible.* The very nature of God within us has a built-in mechanism to desire forgiveness towards others. You are now free to yield to this love, and you're also free from wondering whether you are forgiven or not.

If we pray for God to forgive us based upon how we forgive others, that causes us to wander in the opposite direction of the cross and towards the wrong covenant. Why in the world would we ask God for *conditional* forgiveness when his forgiveness already came unconditionally through the blood of Jesus and his finished work? Think about it ... Jesus performed the will of God with incredible suffering and the shedding of blood on our behalf in order to release us from a hopeless situation. If you think the former covenant still applies and that you can't be forgiven unless you first forgive, for what purpose did Jesus suffer? There would have been no need for him to die if we could have attained forgiveness any other way.

Unfortunately, this leads to the fear of wondering where you stand with God and whether you're truly forgiven because *it places the responsibility back on you instead of Jesus Christ.* Yet this is what people will conclude when covenants collide and context is missing. The law was still in place and not one drop of Christ's blood had yet been shed at the time of this sermon.

Do Not Lead Us Into Temptation: Through the revelation of new covenant Scriptures, we can see it is not God tempting us, and certainly he is not leading us to be tempted or tested with evil or things that cause death and destruction (see James 1:13 & 2 Peter 2:9). Everywhere Jesus went, he was "doing good and healing all who were oppressed by the devil" (Acts 10:38). Jesus was a reflection of God, doing only what the Father would have him do.

Deliver Us from Evil: Under the New Covenant, as confirmed in Colossians 1:13-14 (NKJV), "He has delivered us from the power of darkness and conveyed us into the kingdom of the Son of His love, in whom we have redemption through His blood, the forgiveness of sins."

The same Greek word for *kingdom* is used here in Colossians, and we can see where it is referring to Christ. Therefore, asking to be delivered from something that has already been accomplished just doesn't fit where we are positioned in the New Covenant. As believers, we recognize the enemy has been defeated and we've been delivered from darkness and transferred into the light of Christ. This is a done deal, but shouldn't be confused with the deliverance we are looking forward to when it comes to various afflictions and sufferings experienced in a fallen world (see 2 Corinthians, chapter 1).

It Was an Old Covenant Prayer: With what we've just uncovered about the prayer given to the disciples, there is another common-sense reason we know the target audience for this prayer was for those under the Old Covenant, and not for us today. Other than Jesus using this prayer as it was recorded in Matthew and Luke, there is *never* any mention, instruction, or encouragement by new covenant writers to repeat this prayer. Stop and think about that for a minute. Not once do we hear an apostle suggest we should "pray the prayer the Lord taught us." That's because there would be no need, since *Christ finished and fulfilled everything the prayer would've been seeking.* In other words, for those disciples who prayed in this way, and also in the case of Jesus, when he prayed in the same manner in the garden before his arrest ... their prayers were answered.

Before the cross, Jesus told these people what to pray at *that* time, but he was still using the law to show them where they were positioned under the Old Covenant. That's why they were instructed to pray *in this way*—that God's will be done (the sacrifice of Christ). If that will and testament were not fulfilled, it was going to be like a camel trying to go through the eye of a needle when it came to humankind's redemption.

The Need for Bread

I'd like to throw out one more crumb about the whole bread thing that occurred at another time in the life of Jesus:

> "When the disciples reached the other side, they had forgotten to bring any bread. Jesus said to them, 'Watch and beware of the leaven of the Pharisees and Sadducees.' And they began discussing it among themselves, saying, 'We brought no bread.' But Jesus, aware of this, said, 'O you of little faith, why are you discussing among yourselves the fact that you have no bread?' Then they understood that he did not tell them to beware of the leaven of bread, but of the teaching of the Pharisees and Sadducees" (Matthew 16:5-8, 12).

It's as if Jesus was shaking his head, saying, "What is it with you guys and bread? I told you not to worry about eating."

You certainly have a new take now on the Ten Commandments, but perhaps you haven't heard of the *leaven commandments*. Of course I'm using a play on words, as the eleventh commandment will turn out to be an endless and ever-changing set of rules for you to live by. Number "leaven" will be trumpeted by those who feel called as judge and jury and it will always consist of a new standard for you to live up to. Beware of those who are mixing two covenants together that will result into serving a concoction of *Moses Mash*, mixing it into *Gospel Goulash,* and turning it into a *Christian casserole.* Doing the Moses Mash may be popular in today's churches, but we must not forget it's a graveyard smash—the ministry of death.

Don't Worry about Anything

Moving towards the end of chapter six, in verses 16-24, Jesus continues with what he began saying to his Jewish listeners before the famous prayer by bringing attention to the hypocrisy of openly displaying their self-righteousness. He uses money and the love of it to bring home his point. Attempting to establish their own righteousness for others to see and for them to get noticed was their only reward. Jesus is following the same thread about righteousness that he started the sermon with, and he isn't finished yet.

> "Therefore do not be anxious, saying, 'What shall we eat?' or 'What shall we drink?' or 'What shall we wear?' For the Gentiles seek after all these things, and your heavenly Father knows that you need them all" (Matthew 6:31-32).

God knows people need to eat and have other basic needs in life. He feeds the birds and clothes the flowers, yet you are much more valuable than those. Again, we recognize Jesus is not speaking to Gentiles because of his reference to them eagerly seeking money, food, drink, and clothes. He is reminding these Israelites that the Gentiles will repeat prayers for these things every day, thinking they will be heard if they say them enough.

God's Righteousness

Jesus is trying to get his disciples to stop trying to *earn* a trip on the stairway to heaven by traveling in an outdated, obsolete zeppelin aircraft that can't take them there. He is about to bring home some good news as he reveals the gift that would keep on giving, referring to a new kind of righteousness for his Jewish audience. Contrast what we're about to read with how the sixth chapter of Matthew started out about their own righteousness:

> "But seek first the kingdom of God and his righteousness, and all these things will be added to you" (Matthew 6:33).

Bam! Pow! Kazam! Holy humility, Batman, there it is! Now we're getting somewhere. After nearly two chapters of ministering hopelessness and guilt through the law, the Gowned Crusader is now getting around to the solution—God's righteousness instead of their own. The mystery of God's righteousness for all people was previously hidden, but now has been revealed in the gospel. Matthew 6:33 is another one of those popular verses that wasn't meant for you personally as a believer under the New Covenant. We no longer hunger and thirst for righteousness, nor do we seek the King and his righteousness. Why? *Because we have received his life and have become his righteousness from within.* This wasn't the case for those to whom Jesus was speaking, because the testator had not yet died.

In this covenant of Christ, there is no reason to play the religious game of Hide and Seek with God, because there is no need to search for what is no longer hidden and is already in our possession. With the Lord's Prayer being considered in this context, can you see where it wouldn't make sense for us to seek the kingdom of God while also praying for it to arrive? It had to come in order to be discovered. It's amazing what we'll begin to see when we are able to "zoom out" from the tunnel vision of individual verses, and begin to view chapters, books, and the Bible itself in the context of two different covenants.

When Christians are told they are identified as righteous and perfected, some might ask, "But shouldn't we desire more of God?" To hunger or desire suggests you are craving something you don't possess or are not aware of containing. It sounds religiously correct and it preaches real good, but it lacks the understanding of who we are in him. Avoid letting doubtful thoughts get in the way of your current reality regarding your identity in Christ, and don't confuse bodily hunger that comes and goes with the bread and water of Jesus Christ. Such spiritual cravings will be found only in our own minds, resulting from a lack of understanding when it comes to the finished work. The only pursuit of righteousness for us in the New Covenant is in relationships with other people, along with faith, love, and peace (see 2 Timothy 2:22-23). But the days of chasing after the righteousness of God has ended for those who believe and have called upon his name.

Jesus started out the sermon with the focus on *their* righteousness, but has now revealed something brand new to these Jewish people that they were ignorant of until this point—*God's* righteousness! Jesus the King (of the kingdom) *is* our righteousness, which results in bringing us peace and joy in the Holy Spirit.

(8) THE NARROW GATE (THE SERMON CONCLUDES)

A S THE SERMON CONTINUES in the seventh chapter of Matthew, we find Jesus is still heading in the same direction as when he started. He has just finished telling his Jewish audience to change their thinking from establishing their own righteousness through the law and to begin seeking the King and his righteousness. But as he addresses them on the subject of not judging others, Jesus isn't entirely done with the magnification of what the law says. The Lord is showing them the need to transition from the old way (the law) to the new way (himself). Under the old system, they would be judged by the way they judge others, and by their standard of measure, it would be measured to them. Avoid trying to remove a speck from someone's eye when you have a log in your own. Paul summed it up this way in the context of the works of the law:

> "Therefore you have no excuse, O man, every one of you who judges. For in passing judgment on another you condemn yourself, because you, the judge, practice the very same things" (Romans 2:1).

Therein lies the problem with spiritual referees who always want to blow the whistle on others who commit a penalty and fall short. It's easy to point fingers, especially when trying to abide by law, but watch out, because as soon as you aim that accusation at someone else, a mirror will look right back at you and do the same.

Seeking and Finding

"Ask, and it will be given to you; seek, and you will find; knock, and it will be opened to you. For everyone who asks receives, and the one who seeks finds, and to the one who knocks it will be opened" (Matthew 7:7-8).

Jesus keeps opening the door a little wider to the good news. Shortly before this, recall how he stated not to seek what the Gentiles would seek, such as food and clothes, as God knows your needs before you ask. Yet he says to seek, to knock on the door. We frequently try to apply this to personal, unique situations in our lives, but what is it the Jewish people should seek under the law of the Old Covenant? In context, it would seem he is continuing with what he just got done saying a few verses ago in Matthew 6:33. The first thing they needed to do was to seek the King and his righteousness, and here he continues to talk about seeking and knocking.

"Or which one of you, if his son asks him for bread, will give him a stone? Or if he asks for a fish, will give him a serpent? If you then, who are evil, know how to give good gifts to your children, how much more will your Father who is in heaven give good things to those who ask him!" (Matthew 7:9-11).

When asking the Father for the gift of his Son and his righteousness, he isn't going to turn you away or give you something else that is evil. Luke gets more specific in his writing in Luke 11:13: "If you then, who are evil, know how to give good gifts to your children, how much more will the heavenly Father give the Holy Spirit to those who ask him!"

As the sermon nears its conclusion, Jesus mentions something he started out with, known as the law and the prophets. "So whatever you wish that others would do to you, do also to them, for this is the Law and the Prophets" (Matthew 7:12). It is often called the golden rule, treating others the way you want to be treated. The entire law package revolved around this, and if they could've just followed that *one rule* perfectly, the law and the prophets would be fulfilled. Since nobody had ever accomplished this to the satisfaction of the law, we now find there is a better place to abide, and that is in the one who already fulfilled the law—Jesus Christ.

Jesus is the Gate

"Enter by the narrow gate. For the gate is wide and the way is easy that leads to destruction, and those who enter by it are many. For the gate is narrow and the way is hard that leads to life, and those who find it are few" (Matthew 7:13-14).

Most of us who have been taught a mixture of the two covenants are probably under the impression that the narrow gate is connected to our behavior and lifestyle as we try to live life on "the straight and narrow." Especially if you don't take into consideration the previous two chapters of the sermon in the context of the law, or were under the impression that Jesus was speaking a life application directly to Christians of today. Be assured and comforted that he hasn't been wagging his finger at you in accusation for not doing enough of the right stuff.

So why did Jesus say the way that leads to life is hard? When you have been embedded in a rigorous religious system of works that has defined the way you relate to God as these Jewish people had been, it is very difficult to lay that aside and begin trusting in something (or someone) else. It's often easier for people to continue with their efforts of self-improvement in order to be accepted, even though it only leads to destruction.

The narrow way that leads to life is not a straight and narrow lifestyle; it's the person of Jesus Christ himself. Just as the New Covenant is a person, so is the narrow gate, along with grace, peace, salvation, truth and sanctification. There is only one (narrow) way that leads to life and that is through Jesus, nobody can come to the Father except through him. "I am the door. If anyone enters by me, he will be saved and will go in and out and find pasture" (John 10:9).

Whereas the narrow gate is the person of Jesus Christ, the broad way is the attempt of attaining righteousness through the effort of works that results only in the elevation of the flesh. There are so many ways to show off your religion, because in the land of the legal, it's all about how you want to interpret the rules and even make up some new ones of your own. Broadway Street in New York City is famous for its shows. Performing is a skill the hypocritical Pharisees would use to mesmerize an audience with outward religion to be seen by others, while being rooted in self-righteousness. Jesus addressed this earlier in the sixth chapter of Matthew. It was all for "show" at a place known as the "broad way." So which would you rather have?

Door #1: The guaranteed failure through a system of works, or

Door #2: The guarantee of Jesus Christ (with nothing added).

That was the Day

There is even more to this narrow gate than what appears on the surface. The Psalmist talked about the very same gate with this prophetic passage:

> "Open to me the gates of righteousness, that I may enter through them and give thanks to the LORD. This is the gate of the LORD; the righteous shall enter through it. I thank you that you have answered me and have become my salvation. The stone that the builders rejected has become the cornerstone. This is the LORD's doing; it is marvelous in our eyes" (Psalm 118:19-23).

Look carefully at the connection and consider what Jesus has been talking about—God's righteousness and the narrow gate. In this prophetic Psalm we come to the LORD's gate of righteousness; it's not our gate. This is more than just a poem or a song. It is speaking of an event where the Lord Jesus has become our salvation.

The passage points to Jesus, where believers would find precious salvation, but unbelievers could see only a rock of offense: "The stone that the builders rejected has become the cornerstone ... A stone of stumbling and a rock of offense" (see 1 Peter 2:4-8). This way of righteousness is God's doing (not ours). The Psalm revolves around salvation and righteousness as it looked ahead to the day Jesus would purchase it for us. Waiter, give us the next verse, please:

"This is the day that the LORD has made; let us rejoice and be glad in it" (Psalm 118:24).

As we step away from the trees to see the forest, we'll notice another classic case of a popular Bible verse being taken out of context. How many times have we said (or heard) this verse as referring to *today*? I'm guessing quite a bit. Not that there is anything wrong with being thankful and rejoicing in each day, including today. However, that's not what this Psalm is referencing. "This" day was the one the Lord told his Jewish audience to pray for under the Old Covenant. "The day" the Lord has made that we rejoice in is the day Jesus Christ fulfilled the will of the Father and brought God's righteousness to humankind. The word *made* in the original language here means to accomplish. It is a verb that can imply something that is ordained, observed, and celebrated. The event from this Psalm points to the day the narrow gate of righteousness was opened wide for all to enter through it.

As the Psalm goes on to say, "Blessed is he who comes in the name of the Lord." If the passage sounds familiar, it was shouted by the crowd of people as Jesus made his triumphal entry into Jerusalem riding on a colt. Feel free to thank God for today, but the next time you're singing the song that repeats this verse over and over, remember the bigger picture. Rejoice and be glad in *that* day the Lord has made, because without it, all other days mean nothing.

Fruits From False Prophets

As Jesus continues in verses 15-20 in the seventh chapter of Matthew, he warns of false prophets who appear in sheep's clothing but are ravenous wolves inside. He said *they* would be known by their fruits. This isn't in reference to being able to spot the good guys, but rather to weed out the bad apples who strive to be justified by their own works. There is good fruit and bad fruit, depending on which tree it is coming from. Jesus continues with this:

> "Not everyone who says to me, 'Lord, Lord,' will enter the kingdom of heaven, but the one who does the will of my Father who is in heaven. On that day many will say to me, 'Lord, Lord, did we not prophesy in your name, and cast out demons in your name, and do many mighty works in your name?' And then will I declare to them, 'I never knew you; depart from me, you workers of lawlessness' " (Matthew 7:21–23).

When it comes to doing the will of the Father ... if Jesus had meant a life characterized by obedience to all that was commanded through the law, we would be back under the perfect behavior requirement. The will of God is for us to come to belief in Christ. Again, Jesus has been addressing the subject of false prophets, people found guilty of bragging about all of the good things they did in his name, but would refuse to enter through the narrow gate of Christ alone. Notice they were boasting about some really impressive activities, yet Jesus said that "on that day" he would declare that he *never* knew them. The reason he never knew them is because they never stopped trusting in themselves. You will know them by *their* fruits; this is in contrast to the fruit of the Spirit which is not triggered by our good works, but by God who produces his fruit through us.

This can be connected to the hypocrites Jesus spoke of in the middle of the sermon at the beginning of the sixth chapter of Matthew. While working to establish their own righteousness, their main focus was on the externals, to be seen by others. It's the fruit from the tree of the knowledge of good and evil, not the tree of life. For us who are in Christ, we should recognize we can't perform in a way that will add one jot or tittle to what Jesus did. You've already been perfected! Regardless of how hard we strive, you and I are not the producer of good fruit. We simply rely upon him and his life in us, and we bear the fruit that the Spirit produces through us. Thank God, we have nothing left to boast.

"Then they said to him, 'What must we do, to be doing the works of God?' Jesus answered them, 'This is the work of God, that you believe in him whom he has sent' " (John 6:28–29).

Notice the clash between doing and believing. Inspired by the religious police, all they knew was to do, do, do (de da, da, da). Jesus is telling them that believing is not something they perform, construct or manufacture through their actions, it is "the work of God." The funny thing is ... after Jesus answered them and shut down the "doing" approach, they asked what work *he* would perform so that they may believe. At least now they were getting warmer. Ultimately the work or sign Jesus would give is to spend three days and three nights in the heart of the earth, and then come out of it alive.

In the context of what Jesus said at the end of the sermon, you can cast out demons and perform miracles until you're blue in the face, *but unless you choose to go through the narrow gate by believing in Christ alone, there is no other door available, and you won't be able to find an alternative emergency entrance.*

Finally, it's time to look at the last of this sermon. (I sense people are checking their watches, probably because they have a pork roast in the oven).

> "Everyone then who hears these words of mine and does them will be like a wise man who built his house on the rock. And the rain fell, and the floods came, and the winds blew and beat on that house, but it did not fall, because it had been founded on the rock. And everyone who hears these words of mine and does not do them will be like a foolish man who built his house on the sand" (Matthew 7:24–26).

Keeping in context everything Jesus has talked about in the last three chapters, consider the two foundations he mentioned in the context of the covenants. Build your house on the rock of God's righteousness, the narrow gate. Jesus is that rock, he is that door, and he is the will of God for you. The alternative was to continue down the sandy path of the impossible, unattainable, insurmountable list of rules and regulations that had kept the Jewish people in spiritual bondage those many years. That way is broad without a solid foundation and it can't provide right standing with God. These foundations represent the two covenants.

By the time the sermon was over, the people were struck with shock, awe, and astonishment at the teaching, because it was such a change "from what they had heard" with the law, yet it was communicated with authority. Jesus would go on to fulfill every jot, dot, and tittle of the law on behalf of the people, and he now had his Jewish disciples in a position where they would curiously begin seeking this new gift of God's righteousness, perhaps not yet realizing the gift they would seek stood right before them.

(9) JESUS: GOOD COP, BAD COP

HAVE YOU EVER WONDERED WHY Jesus would seem to come across as rather harsh and heavy at times, while on other occasions he appeared to be more patient and forgiving? Those who have been taught that everything Jesus said was meant for us in a direct, personal way may be wondering if he had a grim twin.

The interrogation method known as good cop/bad cop is where the bad cop takes an aggressive, negative stance towards the subject, whereas the good cop will act sympathetically, appearing supportive and understanding. What may appear as good cop/bad cop scenarios with Jesus is really just a matter of recognizing which covenant is being ministered. It's about becoming aware of whether it was a good news gospel being communicated, or if it was the bad news of impossible requirements directed at Israelites. Watch to see if the communication or command is based on a condition or whether it is unconditional. Both methods had a purpose.

The Rich Young Ruler

When we begin to see the Scripture in the form of the bigger picture, more and more verses and passages will begin to make sense. Let's observe a few examples with the ministry of Jesus beginning with the rich young ruler.

"And behold, a man came up to him, saying, 'Teacher, what good deed must I do to have eternal life?' And he said to him, 'Why do you ask me about what is good? There is only one who is good. If you would enter life, keep the commandments.' He said to him, 'Which ones?' And Jesus said, 'You shall not murder, You shall not commit adultery, You shall not steal, You shall not bear false witness, Honor your father and mother, and, You shall love your neighbor as yourself.' The young man said to him, 'All these I have kept. What do I still lack?' Jesus said to him, 'If you would be perfect, go, sell what you possess and give to the poor, and you will have treasure in heaven; and come, follow me.' When the young man heard this he went away sorrowful, for he had great possessions" (Matthew 19:16–22).

That exchange can be considered a bad cop scenario. Jesus is referring to commandments from the law in the first covenant, which brought death and is now obsolete for us with a different covenant in place. In reference to what Jesus said to this young man, should it be applied to you and me today? Of course not, because that former ministry ended at the cross and was replaced with something new. Am I diminishing the words of Jesus by saying that? No! We can learn from this while gaining a greater grasp of the glorious gospel.

I'll refer to our subject as Mr. Rich Ruler. The fact is that all of the commandments from the law were required to be kept, but Jesus gave Rich just a few samples without even mentioning what he would later call the greatest of the commands. This guy is confident he has kept those commandments from an early age. Jesus knew better but didn't rub his face in it, and it turns out that deep down inside, Rich Ruler *also* knew better. You would think if he had achieved the standard Jesus just gave him, he would've been bouncing off the walls like Daffy Duck shouting, "I'm cuckoo for Cocoa Puffs! Yes! I've kept all those commandments! Woo hoo!" But even after saying he had done all that the law demanded, the young man asked what he was lacking, which can be interpreted as, *what else do I need to do?* This question will still plague everyone who has had religious law embedded in their mind, and it will hound them their entire life until they get free from it.

This young man sincerely came seeking some answers. We find that when Jesus is asked a law-based question he will give a law-based answer. Jesus replied to him in the same way that the question was asked—the man wondered what action he needed to take to obtain eternal life. Keep in mind that there was not a second covenant in effect yet. Jesus is looking at him with compassion, and if you'll allow me to paraphrase, "Okay, my friend, if you want to go back down this broad road of doing, let me repeat the rules." So Jesus accommodated him by referring to his notes from the Sermon on the Mount and let the young ruler know what he lacked.

Rich was missing something that was necessary by the standard of the law—*perfection.* The same Greek word Jesus used for *perfect* at the SOTM is the same one used here in this conversation. Jesus could've used any rule or statute from the law to put this guy down, but he chose just one that would hit the man where he lived in order to bring him to a place where he would be able to see he fell short of the requirement. Imagine being told eternal life would come by keeping the commandments and then receiving confirmation it couldn't be done. This man walked away sad because he wasn't ministered the good news. Have you ever walked out of church feeling worse than when you went in? It was probably for the same reason: the good news was missing.

Law-based religion will always demand more, and you will consistently lack the standard it requires. No matter how well we *think* we've met the standard, there will be no rest under it, because the law doesn't grade on a curve by comparing your performance to those around you. Although Jesus provided us with the gift of life free of charge, without a revelation of the finished work at the cross, man's desire to fix himself by the flesh will still linger.

After speaking to the young ruler, Jesus said it was easier for a camel to go through the eye of a needle than for a rich man to enter the kingdom of God. The disciples were astonished, and they wondered how anyone could make it to heaven if the rich could not be saved. Jesus responded by saying in Matthew 19:26, "With man this is impossible, but with God all things are possible." The exchange between Jesus and this man is not about money or a lack of generosity because it's likely he tithed according to the law, and we don't know whether he may have even given away much more than that. But it still fell short of obtaining the coveted title of "law doer." Regardless of one's resources, by the standard of perfection under the law, everyone was required to surrender all of their possessions and to never turn anyone away who was in need or wanted to borrow. Under the heavy hand of the law in that former covenant, it was impossible for anyone to enter the promise, not just the rich. But the Lord would make it possible for all to enter, through a work that he had yet to accomplish at the time he was speaking to the disciples.

Jesus is ministering the law to someone who thought they had performed good enough to inherit eternal life by having kept the requirements found in the commandments. Yet we see where Mr. Ruler measured that it might not be enough and still wondered "what good deed" could be performed to ensure himself of his own justification. It happens to the best of us when legalism rules our lives: *There must be something more I need to do!* Jesus was attempting to show that Mr. Rich Ruler had not kept the law because if he was truly following the demand of loving others as himself, he would've given everything away and followed Jesus. But here's the clincher: Even if Rich had done all of that, it still would not have been enough.

It may appear as though Jesus is slamming the door shut on this young man, when in fact he was simply trying to open another door to reveal he needed to discover a different way in order to find pasture. If you have a *Jesus Said It* bumper sticker and happen to believe what Jesus said to this rich young ruler about keeping the commandments applies to you, I assume you've already sold everything you possess and have given it away.

The Good Samaritan

One of the more popular parables is that of The Good Samaritan. The title alone implies we may see a story from the good news cop, but if we look closely, we'll see something else at work. Although the phrase "good Samaritan" never appears, it is referenced by the entire world today as a regular person who performs a good or extraordinary deed. A primary reason for its popularity is because it is taught and comprehended in a way that encourages people to contribute something for the good. While this is a wonderful thing to do, the story is actually based upon something else—trying to justify oneself. Before we get to the parable, we need to add a little context as to why Jesus shared it in the first place. He is answering a Jewish law advocate, a citizen who was trying to trick or test him. It was another one of those "what must I do" questions based on the law:

> "And behold, a lawyer stood up to put him to the test, saying, 'Teacher, what shall I do to inherit eternal life?' He said to him, 'What is written in the Law? How do you read it?' And he answered, 'You shall love the Lord your God with all your heart and with all your soul and with all your strength and with all your mind, and your neighbor as yourself.' And he said to him, 'You have answered correctly; do this, and you will live' " (Luke 10:25-28).

If we stopped reading right there and closed the book, we would probably start thinking we needed to carefully comb through the first five books of the Bible to find out more about keeping the Mosaic law in order to earn eternal life. Much like the rich young ruler, this is another case of asking a law-based question and receiving a law-based answer from Jesus, and nobody knew it better than he did. The lawyer may have been a member of the scribes who wanted to see if he could catch Jesus saying something against the law. They were always trying to trap Jesus in this way, because one who denied the law was worthy of death. The Lord essentially told him what he had told the rich young ruler and also the disciples during the SOTM—follow the entire law without failure and do everything perfectly that it demands, including loving God and loving your neighbor as yourself. But notice what the lawyer asks next, which will be what inspires the parable. In trying to justify *himself*, he asked Jesus who his neighbor was, and Jesus replied:

> "A man was going down from Jerusalem to Jericho, and he fell among robbers, who stripped him and beat him and departed, leaving him half dead. Now by chance a priest was going down that road, and when he saw him he passed by on the other side. So likewise a Levite, when he came to the place and saw him, passed

by on the other side. But a Samaritan, as he journeyed, came to where he was, and when he saw him, he had compassion. He went to him and bound up his wounds, pouring on oil and wine. Then he set him on his own animal and brought him to an inn and took care of him. And the next day he took out two denarii and gave them to the innkeeper, saying, 'Take care of him, and whatever more you spend, I will repay you when I come back.' Which of these three, do you think, proved to be a neighbor to the man who fell among the robbers?" He said, 'The one who showed him mercy.' And Jesus said to him, 'You go, and do likewise' " (Luke 10:30-37).

Keep in mind this lawyer is looking for a way to *justify himself* and asked for clarification on who his neighbor was. It must be understood that Jesus was not answering a question about how to treat our neighbors, but was responding to a question about how to inherit eternal life.

Those of us who have been taught a mishmash of Old and New Covenant casserole are going to be looking at this parable from the perspective of *right doing* instead of *right being*. We have been encouraged to take the role of the Samaritan, but by doing so we've missed the message of what Jesus was saying, and have even unknowingly attempted to put ourselves in a position where we take the role and responsibility of Jesus. There is a difference between allowing the Lord to live through us compared with the mistake of pursuing our own justification.

Why did the legalist cross the road? Of course the answer is, *to get to the other side*. The priest who represented the law and passed by the dying man could not address his needs, nor could the Levite who followed after the law. They not only passed by, but went to the other side of the road to do it. One of the reasons for this may have been their concern for the law, which led to the fear of being defiled and considered unclean for many days by having contact with one who was dead. After all, who wants to have the burden of going through the rigorous purification process if it could be avoided, right? The law could not impart life to the one that was dying.

Ladies and gentlemen, please join with me in welcoming to the stage (drum roll) ... the Samaritan in the story, starring Jesus Christ! Self-righteousness yearns to seek the spotlight, but as always, it is Jesus who takes center stage and he represents the Samaritan. The man lying alongside the road represents us—you and me. We were the one who had been robbed by thieves, in a fallen world and without hope, unable to help ourselves and left for dead. Although religion did nothing to help us, the Samaritan did not pass us by, but crossed the road from where he was and came to where we were. Unconcerned about being defiled, he took care of our wounds by pouring oil and wine, symbolic of the Holy Spirit, and brought healing that saved us. As if this wasn't enough, he offered himself to continue to pay for whatever ongoing charges or debt that would be incurred from that point forward with no conditions attached. (If you're looking for someone in the story who is defined as a good Samaritan from the world's perspective, take a closer look at the innkeeper).

The lawyer who inspired the parable asked about how to inherit eternal life, and Jesus knew he was seeking to justify himself. This man who represented the Levite in the parable had tried to use the law to entrap Jesus, but the Lord turned it inside out and ended up catching the guy in his own snare. It was another slam dunk demonstration of Jesus showing that the law could not provide justification or life for us. When Jesus said to *go and do likewise*, the purpose was not so much an exhortation to treat others with mercy, but was yet another magnification of our inability to keep the impossible law. Jesus was telling the lawyer that if he wanted to justify himself, go and do the same *according to the law*. But he would be unable to do it to the perfect standard that the commandment required.

"Do what the law says and you'll have life." Considering this came from Jesus, it sounds good and right, except for one minor flaw; it had never been done! Class was in session and Professor Law was doing the job as the tutor he was meant to be. The Lord had the lawyer between a rock and a sandy place with this parable, and Jesus turned the tables on him faster than you could say, "thou shall not." The point being made to this guy would be something like this: Are you going to follow your interpretation of the law, or will you do what the entire law was wrapped up with in treating your neighbor as yourself? Either way, it left the lawyer speechless and ultimately hopeless.

Am I saying we shouldn't show mercy to others? Of course not, but we don't do it to inherit eternal life. Obviously, it is good to show mercy because mercy triumphs over judgment. It is reasonable to assume the man who was left for dead now had a *genuine* desire to show mercy to others from the inside out. Not because he was commanded to do it or so he could try to acquire mercy in return, but because he received mercy, he could now freely give it.

The Woman Caught in the Act

The religious hypocrites were always watching for an opportunity to accuse Jesus when grace was in action. They would try to use the long arm and pointed finger of the law because they had the view that too much grace wasn't fair and went against the law. Although the ministry of grace is not against the law, it functions apart from the law. The Lord had a way of using their own standard of law against them, such as with the woman who was caught in the act of adultery (see John 8:3-11). It's time for the good news cop. The scribes and Pharisees brought this woman to Jesus while he was teaching at the temple, with the sole purpose of trying to trap him into saying something against the law so they could bring charges against him:

> "The scribes and the Pharisees brought a woman who had been caught in adultery, and placing her in the midst they said to him, 'Teacher, this woman has been caught in the act of adultery. Now in the Law Moses commanded us to stone such women. So what do you say?' " (John 8:3-5).

I'm amazed at how their apparent zeal for the law seemed to inspire such a passion for bloodshed as they eagerly clutched their rocks, when in fact they were just as guilty as the victim. Jesus brilliantly said that whoever was without sin should cast the first stone. We know the story; the accusers filed out one by one beginning with the oldest. It's funny how age brings wisdom just a little bit quicker, not to mention a longer sin resume.

The vultures had been circling this woman, preparing to pounce on one who was about to die. The Dove outsmarted them once again by turning the tables of the law upon them and reminding them that they were judged by the same standard they were judging her. In relation to the commandments, it was a case of killing two stones with one bird. The fact is, the law did call for the woman to be stoned, and by that law they had every right to start throwing rocks even after what Jesus spoke. The law didn't require the "rubble rousers" to be without sin in order to cast their stones. What Jesus did here was a masterful method of tactfully and effectively showing these people they were just as guilty and worthy of punishment as the woman they accused.

Without realizing it, their response was a form of repentance from the covenant they were under. The Lord was demonstrating mercy that would be found in the approaching (new) covenant, yet it was with the use of the law by which he did it. Mercy basically means not getting punishment that is deserved, which is great, but it would lead to something even better— grace! This grace provides us with all the good things found in the life of God through Jesus Christ (that we did nothing to deserve). Grace goes far beyond merely avoiding punishment, after all, grace was upon Jesus and he had never sinned. Grace eternally *empowers* us with God's ability and his very life.

Nobody was left standing there except Jesus and the woman. He had been looking down, writing in the dirt. I can picture Jesus standing up and looking around with his mouth open and a sarcastic look of astonishment while throwing up his arms, "Hey! Where did everybody go? Did *no one* condemn you? Wow, I wonder why! I don't condemn you either. Now go on and stay away from sin such as this."

I love her response when Jesus asked who condemned her and she said, "No one, *Lord*." She knew she had just received a miracle and recognized the Lord Jesus for who he was. When she was told to "go and sin no more," it was not a command from the law as we saw him use against the young ruler and the lawyer. Those chaps erroneously thought they were justified by their law-keeping. Notice the woman wasn't trying to justify herself by boasting of having kept the commands, but instead was snared by them. She never denied guilt and never declared innocence. If Jesus had the intent to minister law to the woman with this statement, his purpose would've been to *show* her condemnation by the futile effort of trying to keep the law's demands. Jesus didn't condemn her with the command, but told her to go and be free of making lousy choices.

Take notice of what Jesus did *not* say to the woman. He didn't threaten her with, "Go and sin no more, *or else!*" He didn't communicate a command attached with a condition such as, "If you don't sin any more, neither will I condemn you." He did not even pull out the most obvious card from his sleeve by saying, "Remember to avoid breaking the seventh commandment." If ever there was a good time to use a commandment written in stone, it would seem as though this was a perfect opportunity. However, by doing so, it would've kept her in bondage, and to use the Apostle Paul's coveting example from the seventh chapter of Romans, it would've led to "all kinds of adultery." Observe how Jesus did not use the commandments to inspire people to avoid sin, because the commandments actually caused sin to increase. He wasn't ministering the law to this woman, but instead was providing a preview of a coming attraction that would come to be known as a better covenant.

The woman had been caught in the act and she was as good as dead, much like the man on the side of the road. But she'd had a personal encounter with The Good Samaritan, where mercy and compassion had been poured out from her Creator and King. He had just freed her from a death sentence and released her from guilt. She wasn't being placed on parole to be released on her own good behavior. The Lord's exhortation here is that she had just been made free, and it would benefit her to avoid biting on the bait of sin that put her in this place, because it would profit her nothing. The young ruler who thought he had set himself apart by keeping the commands walked away sad. On the other hand, this woman was caught breaking them and walked away free. Too bad the guy she had been with wasn't dragged there with her. He missed out on the opportunity of a lifetime.

We're familiar with the famous verse of John 3:16—*God so loved the world*—but in light of the above story, here is what Jesus said next:

> "For God did not send his Son into the world to condemn the world, but in order that the world might be saved through him. Whoever believes in him is not condemned, but whoever does not believe is condemned already, because he has not believed in the name of the only Son of God" (John 3:17-18).

Scripture Sandwiches

To avoid covenant confusion, be mindful of those fast sandwich verses that are squeezed into a passage and can sometimes appear to mean something entirely different by themselves. They are like a drive-thru restaurant, very quick and convenient. Be especially careful when someone orders one of these sandwiches to include "the works," because it will likely be a combo meal from the old *and* new covenant menu. Most assuredly, it will have very little nutritional value and leave you hungering and thirsting for more. Here is a sample of a sandwich where Jesus is speaking to the Pharisees:

> "Everyone who divorces his wife and marries another commits adultery, and he who marries a woman divorced from her husband commits adultery" (Luke 16:18).

Some may consider it amazing how Jesus could pack an entire marriage seminar into a single verse, because he said nothing about the subject of marriage immediately before or after this comment. Leading up to this, Jesus had just shared the prodigal parable and proceeded to address the Pharisees on the law and the prophets, their love of money, and their attempt to justify themselves. The marriage verse is then followed by the story of Lazarus and the rich man, which also ties into the law and the prophets and is compared to believing when someone rises from the dead. If you need a reminder, check out what Paul said in the seventh chapter of Romans regarding the illustration of the Jews' marriage relationship to Professor Law. The law wasn't going to fail and they needed to be freed from their marriage to it. The context of the marriage and divorce comment in the middle of all this has to do with the law and the prophets. How did the story about Lazarus and the rich man end? "He said to him, 'If they do not hear Moses and the Prophets, neither will they be convinced if someone should rise from the dead' " (Luke 16:31).

Jesus does not have a split personality. He is always good. Whenever something in our interpretation seems to contradict the truth about his compassion or his gifts of love, grace and mercy, we should pause to consider who he is speaking to and which covenant is being ministered.

The Kingdom Manifested

A fascinating incident occurred when Jesus told the disciples that some of them would not taste of death until they had seen the kingdom of God after it had come with power. Six days later, Jesus took Peter, James, and John up to a mountain by themselves and he became transfigured, with his clothes turning exceedingly whiter than what any laundry detergent could do. As wild and unexpected as this was, let's pick it up from there:

> "Elijah appeared to them along with Moses; and they were talking with Jesus. Peter said to Jesus, 'Rabbi, it is good for us to be here; let us make three tabernacles, one for You, and one for Moses, and one for Elijah.' For he did not know what to answer; for they became terrified. Then a cloud formed, overshadowing them, and a voice came out of the cloud, 'This is My beloved Son, listen to Him!' All at once they looked around and saw no one with them anymore, except Jesus alone" (Mark 9:4-8 NASB).

Whew! How cool would that have been to witness! I don't imagine those three boys slept real great that night. Good ol' Peter, always trying to be the leader with his spontaneous tabernacle talk. I guess that's what they did back then. Instead of chatting about the weather, one would instinctively fall back on the old stand-by conversation topic of tabernacles. I find it interesting that the disciples knew exactly who Moses and Elijah were, and that was even before social media. With the fear they were experiencing, I can just see Moe, Larry, and Curly looking for a way to scram. I can't say I blame them, and I say it affectionately when I call these disciples the Stooges, because that's how they were viewed by the religious hierarchy. Yet these seemed to be the type of people God would use to the utmost throughout the Scriptures—the type that didn't seem very religious and proper, sometimes uneducated, seemingly unqualified, having a short attention span, and rough around the edges. Yes, everybody loves an underdog.

Peter, James and John saw the kingdom of God manifested. Take a moment to think about what this meant. It wasn't about Moses or Elijah, instead they witnessed the King in a glorified state and the voice of God pointing them to him. The kingdom that has most people today praying for it to come had already arrived in the person of Jesus Christ, and it came with power and glory. What was represented here on this mountain was Moses (the law), Elijah (the prophets), and Jesus (the Messiah and King). Of the three of these, God told the disciples to listen to the Son. Moses and the prophets bore witness to Jesus Christ and he would fulfill them both. When it was all over, there was only one left standing. The two representing the law and the prophets disappeared and were nowhere to be seen. A different covenant was approaching.

(10) THE PRODIGAL CHRONICLES (THE LOST SON UNMASKED)

PERHAPS THE BEST KNOWN PARABLE is the one referred to as The Lost Son or The Prodigal Son. There is something so significant about the message here that I felt it deserved a chapter of its own.

The story begins with a certain man who had two sons. The younger of them asked for his share of the estate and the father divided his wealth between them. The younger son then traveled into a far country and wasted his estate on reckless living, maxed out his credit card, and became in need during a famine in the land. He took a job feeding pigs and was so hungry that he wished he could partake of the pods being fed to the swine. Evidently free chow wasn't included for employees, because nobody gave him anything.

From that point, let's pick up the rest of the story as Jesus tells it, which has been included here for reference purposes. If you haven't looked at the parable lately, I encourage you to read through it before moving ahead because we're about to connect some significant dots, jots, and tittles in the bigger picture.

The Parable

But when he came to himself, he said, "How many of my father's hired servants have more than enough bread, but I perish here with hunger! I will arise and go to my father, and I will say to him, 'Father, I have sinned against heaven and before you. I am no longer worthy to be called your son. Treat me as one of your hired servants.' And he arose and came to his father. But while he was still a long way off, his father saw him and felt compassion, and ran and embraced him and kissed him. And the son said to him, 'Father, I have sinned against heaven and before you. I am no longer worthy to be called your son.' But the father said to his servants, 'Bring quickly the best robe, and put it on him, and put a ring on his hand, and shoes on his feet. And bring the fattened calf and kill it, and let us eat and celebrate. For this my son was dead, and is alive again; he was lost, and is found.' And they began to celebrate.

"Now his older son was in the field, and as he came and drew near to the house, he heard music and dancing. And he called one of the servants and asked what these things meant. And he said to him, 'Your brother has come, and your father has killed the fattened calf, because he has received him back safe and sound.' But he was angry and refused to go in. His father came out and entreated him, but he answered his father, 'Look, these many years I have served you, and I never disobeyed your command, yet you never gave me a young goat that I might celebrate with my friends. But when this son of yours came, who has devoured your property with prostitutes, you killed the fattened calf for him!' And he said to him, 'Son, you are always with me, and all that is mine is yours. It was fitting to celebrate and be glad, for this your brother was dead, and is alive; he was lost, and is found' " (Luke 15:17–32).

* * *

Traditional emphasis on this parable has usually been placed on the son who left home. Many will consciously think of him as a Christian son who went wayward. Others might say he was never saved but left, came back seeking forgiveness, and decided to serve his father with the others from the household. Either way, he sowed his wild oats, ended up blowing his money on wine, women, and song, and starved while watching the pigs eat. Bottom of the barrel for just about anyone. From a works-based perspective, religion continues to put the focus on the younger son, as he decides to "repent of his sins and get right with God." The implication many of us have been taught is that he'll acquire this rightness and forgiveness by returning home to serve, stop doing the bad stuff, and start living with higher morals. A legalistic mindset can't help but think this way. On the way home, the kid was rehearsing his prepared apologetic confession for his dad about how unworthy he was, and how he would come back to serve him.

What happens? He was still *a long way off* (or far off) when the father sees him and runs to him. God ran with compassion to *him*! The son started giving Daddy the sinner's prayer speech he had planned, and the father did not even seem to acknowledge it, but instead he told the wayward son to carry on, offered him peace, and treated him like a king.

My rendition goes like this: "Forget that servant stuff, you're my son, and I'm so glad you are with me. Have yourself a ring, a robe, and a pair of Reeboks. We're breaking out the big heifer. It's party time. Yehaaa!"

The Older Son

Meanwhile, back at the ranch ... the other component to the story is, of course, the older son. This is where it gets interesting. I like to paraphrase, so indulge me. "Hey Pop, I've been here faithfully serving you and never neglecting a single command. Yet I never even once got a young goat to party with my friends, let alone the big heifer. In fact, I had to sacrifice those critters at the altar! Now this kid comes home, hasn't done a dad-blamed thing to earn your respect, and you killed the best chow on the entire spread. It just isn't fair, and I'm not going in!"

You can almost see him crossing his arms as he looks away. Did you notice the self-righteousness manifesting with the older son? He asserted that he had kept every command (law) and actually convinced himself it was true. I can recall someone known as The Rich Young Ruler who had made a similar claim.

There is more to this story than what most of us have realized. *Much more*. We've called this parable The Prodigal Son, which is probably a better title than The Bitter Brother. But I think this parable would be better remembered as *The Faithful Father*, and I'll explain why. It's possible we've missed the entire point of the parable with a mystery that was hidden inside the Father's love since the foundation of the world. If you're a radical grace person and think the older son represents the Christian legalist, I'm going to challenge that. On the other hand, if you've got a traditional mindset as to the younger son being identified as an individual who was separated from God because of his lifestyle choices, that is also out the window.

This parable is taught and expounded upon just about as much as anything else in the Bible. I've heard a lot of interesting extractions and insights through the attempts at teaching what can be learned from the parable, and it seems to be a bottomless well of various thoughts and viewpoints, whether it be from a standpoint of legalism or grace. Let's step back from the trees for a better view of the forest in order to gain a larger perspective that I think traditional teaching has missed.

Most will agree that the father in the parable represents God. He has two sons—which is interesting, since there are so many in all of creation—but why two sons? It should make us pause and ask who these two sons were. Who was it the Father's love was specifically reaching out to in this instance? Certainly it was *both* sons, but if the father in the story is God, who do the two sons represent? There is a reason why we have mentioned Gentiles quite frequently so far, and it has brought us to this place.

Far Off

It's easy to understand why we keep coming up with new ways to relate this story to our lives as long as we are looking at these two sons in the story as individuals. However, I don't believe the sons are meant to be viewed as individuals, but rather two *groups*. Consider it is the younger son who represents the race of those despised Gentiles, and the older son represents the Jewish race of Israel. How is it that we would come to this conclusion? The lost son was *far off* when his father ran to him. Compare this to something the Apostle Paul referred to in the second chapter of Ephesians, and it's important to mention he is addressing Gentiles:

> "Remember that you were at that time separated from Christ, alienated from the commonwealth of Israel and strangers to the

covenants of promise, having no hope and without God in the world. But now in Christ Jesus you who once were far off have been brought near by the blood of Christ" (Ephesians 2:12-13).

With this *far off* reference, Paul used the same Greek word as was used in the parable (also translated a long way off). We Gentiles who were formerly "far off" have now been brought near by the blood of Christ. Paul continues to explain what all of this means for the two groups:

"For he himself is our peace, who has made us both one and has broken down in his flesh the dividing wall of hostility by abolishing the law of commandments expressed in ordinances, that he might create in himself one new man in place of the two, so making peace, and might reconcile us both to God in one body through the cross, thereby killing the hostility" (Ephesians 2:14-16).

Jew and Gentile both now have peace, and the two groups were made into "one man" because Christ broke down the barrier, or dividing wall. And what was that barrier? *The law of commandments expressed in ordinances.* This barrier had kept the Jews in bondage within the previous covenant, and it kept Gentiles far off with no covenant at all.

Together As One

Paul continues to explain what occurred between Jews and Gentiles as a result of the dividing wall being broken down:

"And he came and preached peace to you who were far off and peace to those who were near. For through him we both have access in one Spirit to the Father. So then you are no longer strangers and aliens, but you are fellow citizens with the saints and members of the household of God ..." (Ephesians 2:17-19).

Gentiles were made to be one with the Jewish people, and we now have access to the same Father, and we belong in the same household. Look carefully and see the connection between this truth and our parable.

Remember that the older, more experienced son said, "I've served you for so many years and never neglected a command." God pleaded with him to celebrate, and reminded him that he had always been with him. The father in the parable attempted to explain the situation where the younger brother had been considered dead, but was now alive; was lost but now found. God speaking to the older son is an example Paul used in Ephesians where peace was preached or shared with those who were near (the Jews). He did the same with the younger Gentile son who had been far away.

The book of Ephesians was a letter written to Gentiles. From here, Paul went on to say a mystery had been revealed to him in the Spirit and to other apostles and prophets that had not been revealed in previous generations. What was the mystery? He said, "This mystery is that the Gentiles are fellow heirs, members of the same body, and partakers of the promise in Christ Jesus through the gospel" (Ephesians 3:6).

That was a tough one for many of the Jews to absorb at first, as was demonstrated in the book of Acts and in the story of the elder son in the parable. Put yourself in their sandals for a moment. Consider all the difficulties the Jewish people had been through, including the work and toil, the persecution, the sacrifices and rule keeping. Ponder the special chosen connection they had with the Almighty through their covenant and heritage. They were supposed to be the chosen ones, and now Daddy just adopted this wayward child into the family as one of his own. These immoral, unclean Gentiles did nothing to deserve it. They had absolutely no relationship to the cherished holy laws that were held in such high esteem by the nation of Israel, the nation that had been the salt of the earth and the light of the world. To them, this may have been the equivalent of inviting the hyenas to live with the lions in their pride from the movie, *The Lion King*. You'd better believe there was plenty of pride, and it was hard to swallow.

Grace just doesn't seem fair to those who have tried so hard to serve. That's what frustrated the eldest son in the parable who represented Israel. It struck him as wrong and unlawful that the younger brother should be allowed off of sin's hook without having to pay some sort of price. But no penance or sacrifice was required. This Gentile brother wasn't even *pursuing* right standing with God as the older son had been all those years;

instead, righteousness ran to the kid! It was hard for him to understand how the younger one had somehow attained right standing with the Father by grace through faith alone without having to establish himself. The older son had not yet grasped that he had been given the same gift of life and acceptance that the law could not provide. With faith established and the promise available to receive, he would no longer be held as if he were a prisoner under the command.

They celebrated by eating, and had fellowship and communion with the Father without a priest in sight! What a contrast between the law that came through Moses and the grace and truth that came through Jesus Christ. The gospel of peace now proclaimed to both those who were near (Jews) and those who had been far away (Gentiles). The father in the story reached out to his older son to make sure he knew he was still a part of the family and was welcome into the house as he always had been, and he pleaded with him to join in the fellowship and celebration. But the Jewish brother refused to go in.

The older son's response of rejecting the New Covenant is something Jesus shared in the thirteenth and fourteenth chapters of Luke, preceding the parable of The Lost Son. That parable is part of a string of parables held together in the context of Israel's rejection of the Messiah and the offer to outsiders being invited to the table. As we go back one chapter, we find an example with The Parable of the Dinner (also called The Great Supper), where the Jewish people rejected the invitation to enter and made up excuses as to why they would not attend the dinner. Let's pick it up from there:

> "So the servant came and reported these things to his master. Then the master of the house became angry and said to his servant, 'Go out quickly to the streets and lanes of the city, and bring in the poor and crippled and blind and lame.' And the servant said, 'Sir, what you commanded has been done, and still there is room.' And the master said to the servant, 'Go out to the highways and hedges and compel people to come in, that my house may be filled. For I tell you, none of those men who were invited shall taste my banquet" (Luke 14:21–24).

Israel had declined the invitation, so the welcome message was extended beyond the highways and the hedges, to others who had often been considered less desirable or unworthy. There's a huge connection to be made here—the word *hedges* is defined as a fence or partition (Strong's G5418). In other words, it was something that separates and prevents two from coming together. It is the same word translated *dividing wall* that we saw in the second chapter of Ephesians, referring to the law and the commandments that Jesus broke down so Gentiles could abide in God's household. Compare this to the older Jewish brother in the parable who refused to go into the house. Those without the means to repay—the poor, the crippled, the blind or lame, and also Gentiles from all directions—were invited into *the house*, and not just the house of Israel, but the house of God.

Since the beginning as God's creation, I would suggest Gentiles had never stopped being children any less than the Israelites; they just weren't part of that chosen nation by which God would fulfill his will for the entire world. Perhaps through the eyes of the law they were viewed as unclean animals. But through the eyes of God, I think this parable shows that Gentiles were children, although lost in darkness and not in a covenant with God. They were ignorant, estranged, and not part of the household, but that did not make them any less loved by the Lord. At one time, Gentiles went their separate ways, and Israel became a chosen nation through which God would fulfill his will and purpose. The Gentiles were far off in another land, without hope and void of the one true God in the world, just like the lost son. Along the way, he became cold as ice, a foreigner who was a long, long way from home, one who developed double vision and wanted to know what love is. But in due time the welcome invitations to the heavenly dinner were sent out to all:

> "There is neither Jew nor Greek, there is neither slave nor free, there is no male and female, for you are all one in Christ Jesus. And if you are Christ's, then you are Abraham's offspring, heirs according to promise" (Galatians 3:28-29).

Religion will often take the eleventh chapter of Romans out of context and teach that Gentiles were grafted into Israel, but this is misleading. The second chapter of Ephesians clearly shows both Jew and Gentile were grafted or brought *into Christ* so that God might make the two into one new man and reconcile them in one body. Which body? The body of Jesus Christ, who fulfilled the law and through the cross put to death the enmity, or that which had alienated us. This is the mystery of the new and better covenant which we have all been invited into (see Romans 11:25–27).

The Jewish race had the advantage of being set apart at one time and used by God in an extraordinary way, but now that separation with the rest of the world has been broken down. God desired to reveal the knowledge of his will which had formerly been a hidden mystery. What was it? Christ in you, the hope of glory. That is, Christ in you *Gentiles*:

> "The mystery which has been hidden from the past ages and generations, but has now been manifested to His saints, to whom God willed to make known what is the riches of the glory of this mystery among the Gentiles, which is Christ in you, the hope of glory" (Colossians 1:26–27 NASB).

In Christ, we are no longer lost, prodigal, wayward children. While sin is always wise to avoid, Jesus dealt with its penalty, and it will never come between us and our relationship with the Lord ever again. Now Gentiles are forever part of the household of God, because the barrier of law and commandments was broken down and taken out of the way. We no longer leave the house and drift away, only to return when we feel a sense of separation. That occurred once upon a time, long ago, in a land far, far away.

PART 3: COVENANT CONCLUSION

There is a difference between trying to abide by law and rules, compared to living by the indwelling Christ in us. Bearing fruit to God came through having died to the law and being joined to Christ. The objective is no longer centered on trying to avoid evil and doing good, but our purpose is to intimately know Jesus Christ and the power of his resurrection.

Part 3 Overview:

A. God has already dealt with the issue of forgiveness, once for all.
B. Tithing, giving, repentance.
C. Living the life of Christ.

(11) THE FORGIVENESS BUSINESS

HAVE I GONE TOO FAR TO BE FORGIVEN? That was the subject line of an email someone had written to our podcast ministry. It was a long correspondence in which she shared the difficult situations she had endured since being abused as a child and through the many challenges of her adult years. The pain and agony could be felt in her words as she desperately wanted to know if she had crossed a line from which she could never return. She stated she believed in Jesus Christ, but now felt enveloped by fear and was beginning to doubt her salvation. She wrote, "I seem to be comforted by my Christian friend for a short time, then the fear returns. It is a blackness that I can't describe, filled with hopelessness and despair. Will God abandon me? Has he already left?"

As sad as this is for her to be experiencing this anguish, it's even more troubling that it was birthed through the ministry of religious Bible teaching she heard on the radio from a nationally known pastor and theologian. While barely left with only a crumb of blessed assurance, she was being told the very opposite of what the Spirit will bear witness to her—that she is a child of the living God. The enemy will take this kind of lifeless seed and attempt to cultivate it into fear, if our minds allow it. In the new and everlasting covenant, our focus shouldn't be on asking the question as to whether God will forgive, but rather we ought to fix our eyes on the answer that he has already completely forgiven through the cross.

Many have lived in fear of wondering whether God has elected to accept them into his grand, eternal plan. Here's the good news: God isn't picking winners and losers; we have *all* been predestined to receive an inheritance as children, both Jew and Gentile. Therefore, the question is *not* whether God has chosen you (he already has), but whether you will choose him by believing, instead of trusting in your own works. The choice belongs to you. This isn't a work on our part but a simple response from the heart.

In Christ we have been reconciled, which means he *exchanged* our nature of sin for his holy nature of righteousness within our spirits. As confirmed in 2 Corinthians 5:19, "... in Christ God was reconciling the world to himself, not counting their trespasses against them, and entrusting to us the message of reconciliation."

The Psalmist looked forward to the time of Christ, where God would not deal with us according to our sins, which were to be removed and remembered no more:

> "He does not deal with us according to our sins, nor repay us according to our iniquities. For as high as the heavens are above the earth, so great is his steadfast love toward those who fear him; as far as the east is from the west, so far does he remove our transgressions from us" (Psalm 103:10-12).

You may have heard the old saying, "Go West, young man." If you start heading west and keep going, you will never be moving in an easterly direction; the distance between east and west is infinite and they will never meet.

Here's a really wild thought—suppose God actually meant what he said when it comes to no longer remembering our sins, not counting them against us, and isn't dealing with us according to our sins. If this is absolutely true, it changes everything. Of course it *is* true! When we think about the magnitude of this, it should bring a sigh of relief and the response of great rejoicing and celebration.

"But you don't know what I've done!" I can't begin to tell you how many times I've heard a line like that over the years. I don't need to know what you've *done*—I know what Jesus *did*.

Forgiveness is Complete

I know this will sound radical to those who have been stuck in Moses mode, but God has already addressed our need for forgiveness through the payment of the blood of Jesus Christ, and there is no amount of effort through our doing that we can contribute to the cause. At the very heart of our thinking we need to do something in order to get God to respond with another act of forgiveness again and again is an old covenant concept dressed in new covenant clothes. Here is the key to unlocking the door of the prison cell that it took me many years to discover: *The finished work of Christ dealt with all sins; past, present and future.* If this is not the case, then we're all doomed, because he performed only one sacrifice. If it was not sufficient, that's bad news, because there is no further blood being shed to bring more redemption and more forgiveness.

I can imagine the wheels spinning in peoples' minds everywhere as they wonder why they haven't heard this before, especially after being in church for so long. Imagine the devastating blow to the religious industry if something like this were to ever be made public! Indeed, there was a Jesus revolution which brought a recession to the religious economy after the cross, and it caused numerous layoffs in the Jewish priesthood. Eventually it had to shut down, but it didn't take long for another company of religious entrepreneurs to step in and "revive" that economy by putting people back to "works." The business of forgiveness has allowed religious authorities to ensure themselves of repeated patronage from their "customers" who will still feel the need to depend upon them, and therefore will remain under their control.

Covenant clashers will level the charge that we are wading into murky waters by being so bold about God's forgiveness. They will sound the alarm to warn the sheep of what they consider to be a message of dangerous grace. In doing so, without realizing it, they have diluted the power of the blood of Jesus Christ and the finished work of the cross.

If the forgiveness for sins from God is *not* yet complete, and we were only forgiven up to this moment due to a certain measure of law still in place, blood would have to keep being spilled just as it was under the law of the Jewish priests. As we learn in Hebrews 9:22, "Indeed, under the law almost everything is purified with blood, and without the shedding of blood there is no forgiveness of sins."

If sin has not been put away forever and forgiveness wasn't completely addressed by the shedding of Christ's blood, this would mean when someone commits another sin, Jesus would need to offer himself again and again (see Hebrews 9:26). However, his sacrifice, which was offered once and for all, dealt with the issue of sin ever coming between God and man again, and this is confirmed in Hebrews 10:18: "Where there is forgiveness of these, there is no longer any offering for sin."

The writer of Hebrews was explaining to Jewish people that the old system which included repeated sacrifices, had been abolished and rendered idle. As we stay in context, he went on to share this nugget that is often misunderstood: "For if we go on sinning willfully after receiving the knowledge of the truth, there no longer remains a sacrifice for sins" (Hebrews 10:26 NASB). It sounds a little scary by itself, but when considering the context leading up to it (including verse 18), the crux of what is being said here is that if the activity of sin continues to occur, and you reject *the one and only* sacrifice that God has provided, there no longer remains a sacrifice for sins. The only thing you would have to look forward to is the judgment of wrath.

The same person who wrote to this group of Hebrews in the referenced 10:26, had previously shared that Jesus Christ was the guarantee of a better covenant. Unlike the former priests under the law who died, he continues forever with a permanent priesthood and he is able to save *forever*. Jesus lives to make intercession and blocks the sin problem between us and God (see Hebrews 7). *The warning about "willful sin" was not directed at people who sin, but rather at people who reject the sacrifice of Jesus as the only offering that takes away all their sin.* The Hebrew people who received this letter understood the message here was very different than what they had previously held onto—*it was a word of grace.*

This is a stark difference between the former covenant and the new one. God isn't going to double-cross us by having Jesus return to offer another sacrifice, or another one after that. Neither is it like another nail being driven into the hands of Jesus when a sin is committed. Jesus *became* sin for us and destroyed it with his one-time sacrifice at the cross in order to bring eternal satisfaction to the Father.

Try to avoid getting lost and disoriented while hiking through a forest of individual Bible verses, but instead mark your territory in order to become more aware of your surroundings, and connect to a path that will lead to a place of safety and a better understanding of the truth. Don't allow the ministry of legalism to deposit fear into your mind with a single verse interpreted out of context that implies salvation is dependent upon your performance.

Change of Priesthood: Change of Law

In the previous covenant, sins would linger because those sacrifices could not remove them. However, when the sins are taken away, the sacrifices stop.

> "For since the law has but a shadow of the good things to come instead of the true form of these realities, it can never, by the same sacrifices that are continually offered every year, make perfect those who draw near. Otherwise, would they not have ceased to be offered, since the worshipers, having once been cleansed, would no longer have any consciousness of sins? But in these sacrifices there is a reminder of sins every year. For it is impossible for the blood of bulls and goats to take away sins" (Hebrews 10:1-4).

The book of Hebrews explains that, under the previous covenant, every high priest ministered with gifts and sacrifices according to the law given through Moses. They stood and ministered daily, offering the same sacrifices that could *never* take away sins. There wasn't a labor union representing priests on this "assembly" line, therefore no lounge or coffee breaks were permitted in the temple, because the priests would not be allowed to sit, but had to keep standing. Why? It's simple—the job was never finished:

> "Every priest stands daily ministering and offering time after time the same sacrifices, which can never take away sins; but He, having offered one sacrifice for sins for all time, sat down at the right hand of God, waiting from that time onward until His

enemies be made a footstool for his feet" (Hebrews 10:11-13 NASB).

Our High Priest didn't just take a bow, he sat down. There will be no encore and no second act, so don't expect a curtain call, because the temple's curtain was torn in two after the ultimate sacrifice.

Before the cross, as long as people kept sinning, priests would have to keep sacrificing for the atonement of those sins. By the way, the priests also offered up sacrifices for their *own* sins as well as those of the people. All of this brought a constant reminder of sins and burdened the people with a sin consciousness of guilt from which they couldn't escape, and it could only provide a temporary atonement. The word *atonement* is an Old Testament word that means a covering. Their sins were covered by the blood of the animals but not removed.

In order to be delivered from this dilemma, *a change of priesthood would need to occur,* and *all* of the old law had to be entirely replaced with something new, as confirmed in Hebrews 7:12: "For when there is a change in the priesthood, there is necessarily a change in the law as well." This is huge! The word *change* in this instance means "change, transformation, removal, desert, transfer" (Strong's G3331 and G3346). In other words, the change of law that occurred wasn't a *revision* of the existing law; it was withdrawn, removed and abandoned. There would be an immediate transfer from one covenant to another, as something brand new was established. If this is not the case, then Jesus could not claim the title of high priest.

It wasn't God who changed, he has always remained the same, but the way that we are able to fellowship with him is because the old system of law was completely changed and put away. Here is more proof of this truth:

> "For the one of whom these things are spoken belonged to another tribe, from which no one has ever served at the altar. For it is evident that our Lord was descended from Judah, and in connection with that tribe Moses said nothing about priests" (Hebrews 7:13-14).

All priests under the law came from the tribe of Levi. Yet Jesus descended from the tribe of Judah. Again, if the old law with its commands are still in effect, Jesus cannot be considered a bona fide high priest.

> "For on the one hand, a former commandment is set aside because of its weakness and uselessness (for the law made nothing perfect); but on the other hand, a better hope is introduced, through which we draw near to God" (Hebrews 7:18-19).

Since the former command from the first covenant was weak and useless for bringing life to the Israelites, wouldn't it be silly to try to apply it to our lives today? Sure it would, especially considering it was put away and made obsolete. With a better hope, established upon better promises, it makes no sense for us to apply portions of a covenant to our lives that failed to bring the promise.

Under the Old Covenant, there were many high priests who were appointed to their position by the law and not with an oath. They would remain priests for a certain number of years or until they died, and then other priests would take over. On the other hand, our (one) high priest, Jesus Christ, wasn't appointed by the law but came to his position through an oath (or promise) from the Father.

> "For the Law appoints men as high priests who are weak, but the word of the oath, which came after the Law, appoints a Son, made perfect forever" (Hebrews 7:28 NASB).

When did the word of the oath come to appoint Jesus as High Priest forever? *It came after the law.* When did that occur? *After the death of the testator (Jesus).* Unlike the priests before him, Jesus lives forever and has established a permanent priesthood.

If you still want to believe the Old Covenant is in place to be mixed with the New, and that both Jews and Gentiles are required to keep fragments of the law, you'll have to stick to the old priesthood of men. Too bad it won't do you any good, though. You see, as earthly priests, they have no power to take away sins. Jesus came to do God's will and get rid of all those copies and shadows of the real thing, and he has become the *only* mediator between us and God (see 1 Timothy 2:5).

Following the fall of humankind, we get an early glimpse into what would be considered an acceptable offering to God. It is likely God demonstrated the first blood sacrifice in the presence of Adam and his wife when he made garments of skin to clothe them (see Genesis 3:21). In the next chapter, we see where Abel's offering included blood, whereas Cain brought the fruit of his own labor. God regarded Abel's offering, but not Cain's. The first legalist on record blamed the other guy for making him look bad and decided to kill him. Our works and efforts have nothing to do with redemption, but redemption has everything to do with the blood of the cross of Christ.

Animal sacrifices and burnt offerings which were offered according to the law, were never the will of God, who took no pleasure in them (see Hebrews 10:8). This is interesting when considering it was *God* who introduced them long before the law and they became part of the covenant that the nation of Israel agreed upon. But it was all meant to point them to Christ because those sacrifices were not the permanent solution. They were just a copy or shadow of the one and only sacrifice of Christ that would bring redemption.

Don't let anyone mislead you into thinking Jesus was murdered and that the sacrifice of Christ was unnecessary. Nobody takes away the life of God ... Jesus willingly laid it down and he took it back up again (see John 10:18). God wasn't attempting to appease the Jewish people with a crucifixion in order to more effectively relate to their sacrificial culture. This was a plan put into place by God *before the foundation of the world*. Earthly sacrifices were a shadow of something heavenly, not the other way around.

Allow me just one paragraph to step aside for a quick timeout. Although legalists will wrongly try to use fear as a recruitment tool, I'm aware of certain factions within the grace community who will try to dance around the subject of the wrath of God. They seem to feel it is contradictory to speak of love and wrath coming from the same source. This is a topic deserving a separate book of its own, but I'll just say this about the subject ... the wrath of a holy and righteous God is not against *you*, it's clearly against sin itself. This brings us back to the good news of Christ's finished work: "For the law brings wrath, but where there is no law there is no transgression" (Romans 4:15). God demonstrated his love by Christ dying for us, while we were still defined as sinners, and fully delivered us from the sin problem, saving us from his wrath (see Romans 5:8-9).

In grace, we don't take sin lightly. We recognize it for the terrible thing that it is, missing the mark of God's holiness and righteousness. Make no mistake—sin causes pain, it hurts people, and it affects others around them. Often the poor decisions we make can upset our circumstances in this life and may have a ripple effect on various situations. But in Christ, we also recognize that God doesn't punish us for our sins because he took care of the problem completely by having Jesus crushed for our iniquities, and it pleased him to do so (see Isaiah 53:10). God is just *and* he is the justifier. Consequences for our choices may impact our life in *this* world. However, in regards to the problem with our eternal justification, God *dealt* with it.

Over the years, I've observed how those trapped within a modern-day form of old covenant legalism will become so easily offended over the subject of free grace and the concept of once-for-all forgiveness. Frankly, it astounds me. It might cause one to wonder if the last words of Jesus on the cross were "It is *not* finished." Much like the Israelites, our pride desires for us to be included in the formula and be a part of the equation. Fortunately for us, this was a recipe that would include just a couple of ingredients—God and himself (see Hebrews 6:13). We simply can't mess up this blood covenant between the Father and the Son. We have an assurance or a guarantee that it can't fail because he could swear by no one greater.

Sanctification as a Gift

In the land of the legal, there is a common mindset that salvation is a free gift, but being sanctified is our responsibility. To be *sanctified* basically means to be made holy and set apart. For covenant clashers, this can mean grace plus works, or sometimes the other way around. After all, ever since the Garden of Eden, well-meaning humans can't resist the temptation of thinking self-improvement will bring them closer and make them more acceptable to God. Similar to forgiveness, sanctification has become big business in the world of legalistic religion. The effort to become sanctified develops into a long and frustrating process where your works and lifestyle begin to take center stage as you try to improve and move up to the next spiritual level—a level that doesn't exist. This ongoing endeavor will cause the pursuit of attempting to *maintain* fellowship and right standing with God. Those of us who believe in faith-based righteousness are of the persuasion that Jesus Christ did it all for us, doing what we were not capable of achieving.

Where religion has gotten this wrong is by confusing behavior with sanctification. God has already done the work to set us apart and has dedicated us in Christ. Jesus said he sanctified himself so we could be sanctified in the truth of his word (see John 17). This isn't a progressive process, but a completed task from the shed blood of Jesus Christ at the cross. Certainly our behavioral changes and how we conduct ourselves are progressive (see 1 Peter 1:15). However, in Christ we are not identified or defined by our behavior. Recognizing who you've already been made to be will potentially trigger a positive response in behavior, but how you yield to good or bad choices is not a guarantee. *Jesus is our guarantee.* We shouldn't confuse our new identity with our actions, remembering that we are children of God through a new spiritual birth, not because of behavior improvement. We are set apart only by faith in Jesus Christ (see Acts 26:18).

In the gospel of grace, sanctification is defined as a gift, and it was part of the will of God that was completed through the offering of the body of Jesus Christ: "By this will we have been sanctified through the offering of the body of Jesus Christ once for all. For by one offering He has perfected for all time those who are sanctified" (Hebrews 10:10, 14 NASB).

Some translations have added the word *being* before "sanctified" at the end of verse 14, but it is the only place where you'll see this in the New Testament. Earlier in this passage, it is clearly stated he *has* brought perfection to us by his single sacrifice, not by our doing. This is in contrast to the progressive attempts under the law of the first covenant, which could not bring perfection (see Hebrews 7:19, 9:9, 10:1). Therefore, even if you believe the word *being* was correctly added, a consistent interpretation should recognize the word can simply be defined as something that exists.

If sanctification is a work in progress, we have contradictions in the Scripture. Although mixed covenant teaching will often agree that we're *justified* by faith, it argues that only partial sanctification has occurred thus far, and it is our responsibility and even our obligation to participate in finishing that part of the process. Yet Paul said something quite different: "And such were some of you. But you were washed, you were sanctified, you were justified in the name of the Lord Jesus Christ and by the Spirit of our God" (1 Corinthians 6:11).

This is not something we are waiting patiently to occur later in the sweet by and by. "You were" shows us these things have already been completed in us and are part of a *new package* in the covenant of grace. If we're progressing towards attaining or even *maintaining* either sanctification or salvation, then we're back under works, and we know that's a dead-end street. Christ Jesus *became* our sanctification once and for all, and it's time to concede we can add nothing to the work that Jesus finished. Regardless of what you've been told by the controlling powers in the land of the legal, *sanctification cannot be defined outside of what God did in Jesus Christ on our behalf.* With that in mind, take a look at this powerful and precious cargo Paul delivered to the church in Corinth:

> "And because of him you are in Christ Jesus, who became to us wisdom from God, righteousness and sanctification and redemption, so that, as it is written, 'Let the one who boasts, boast in the Lord' " (1 Corinthians 1:30-31).

Hopefully you caught the magnitude of that last passage—Jesus became our righteousness, sanctification, and redemption. Religious flesh will feel the need to be credited for something that was done in order to attain some sort of recognition. We've been credited alright, but as it was for Abraham, the same is true for us; it is the *gift* of righteousness with which we've been credited, received through belief (see Romans 4:3).

In spite of all the passages related to our completed sanctification in Jesus Christ, legalists love to scour the Bible for a single verse that appears to put the responsibility back on us again because it's good for the religious business. Here is an example from Hebrews 12:14 (NASB): "Pursue peace with all men, and the sanctification without which no one will see the Lord." Many translations use the word holiness in place of sanctification.

The exhortation here isn't to try harder at becoming what you are not, but to press towards living outwardly in a way that reflects the new inward reality of who you have already been identified and created to be by the grace of God. The twelfth chapter of Hebrews begins with the example of us running the race by turning our eyes away from the distractions and keeping them fixed on Jesus. He is the perfecter of faith, not us.

Since no one will see the Lord without holiness or sanctification, it sure is good to know it's not up to you and me to achieve this status. The writer of Hebrews had already addressed the people he was writing to as holy (see Hebrews 3:1). The rest of the letter proceeds to describe the superiority of Christ compared to the law found in the first covenant. When the old system came to an end, sin and sacrifices were removed, while the people were sanctified and perfected through what Jesus did.

Another "verse" that gets pounded into us in order to promote progressive sanctification is this one:

> "Now may the God of peace himself sanctify you completely, and may your whole spirit and soul and body be kept blameless at the coming of our Lord Jesus Christ. He who calls you is faithful; he will surely do it" (1 Thessalonians 5:23).

Since God has declared us righteous already, this would mean we're also blameless in his eyes. The previous verse (22) encourages us to avoid every form of evil. This is speaking of behavior that is seen outwardly, and it is advising us to avoid evil in order to remain blameless *in the eyes of other people.* Behavior improvement is progressive, but religion is constantly confusing this with your true, spiritual identity. God is the one who is faithful and he is the doer when it comes to being sanctified both inwardly and outwardly.

I often experience a spontaneous reflex of shaking my head and rolling my eyes when I hear the word "positional" being tossed around loosely, as if it's actually something that is clearly communicated in the New Covenant. Hey, I get it. We *are* positioned in a special place in Christ. But don't believe the religious script that says you're still just a rotten sinner and that God only "sees" you as righteous. Oh sure, you'll hear plenty of convincing theology about positional holiness, righteousness and sanctification. You'll be coaxed into thinking these gifts that were provided through the work of Christ will be perfected by the "process" of behavior improvement. Do they really believe people can perfect what God started by their own works? This will frequently result in us striving to do what Israel could not accomplish through the law—the attempt of acquiring an improved position with God by ignorantly trying to establish *our own* righteousness, holiness and sanctification.

Peter exhorted us to "grow in the grace and knowledge of our Lord and Savior Jesus Christ" (see 2 Peter 3:18). To grow in the grace and knowledge of Jesus Christ is to gain a greater understanding of our existing identity in him and the fullness of his redemptive work. He has brought us peace and we're found to be spotless and blameless in him. As Peter stated in this passage, these things that the Apostle Paul spoke about in his writings can be hard to understand and the misguided will distort them, as they do the rest of the Scriptures. Although you may never achieve perfection in all that you do, you *have been* perfected! God did it! This is the truth we live in—the reality of life in Christ. Now go ahead and allow your outward behavior to be a reflection of who you already are.

It's just plain silly to think we can become more holy than what God has already made us to be in Christ by striving for a higher level of morality. Nobody has ever consistently achieved holiness in *all* their behavior. This was a requirement God spoke to the Jews when the law was given to them. Our actions may mirror God's holiness at times because of who we've been created to be through an imperishable inheritance that brought us grace and peace by the blood of Jesus (see 1 Peter 1:1-19). But the reason we're able to "be holy" is because God is already holy and dwells within us. *It's a good thing to live in a way that avoids sin and demonstrates the goodness of God within us.* The point I'm making is that our good or bad behavioral choices should not be confused with how God identifies us as children who have been born into his family, and are already declared righteous, holy and set apart.

The reason for our existing justification *and* sanctification is *because* we're in Christ, not as the result of our ability to maintain some sort of level of good works, principles or dedication we think is acceptable. We hear a lot about Christ being in us, which is good and true, yet there are substantially more references in Scripture to us being in Christ. As a reminder, we just need to ask ourselves whether Jesus is holy, perfect, and righteous. We know the answer is yes, and we just saw where he is also sanctified. Since we are in him, we are also all of these things, "because as he is so also are we in this world" (1 John 4:17).

The Blood Brought Forgiveness

The driving force in the economy of God's kingdom is blood. The blood of Christ was needed only once and it finished what the law could not do. To see for yourself the certainty of your forgiveness, here are just a few stops you can make when traveling through Scripture: Colossians 1:13, 2:13-14; Ephesians 1:7; 1 John 2:12. These passages declare he *has* forgiven us all our transgressions, and be mindful that this forgiveness occurred through his blood.

John introduced Jesus as "the Lamb of God who takes away the sins of the world" (John 1:29). Not only did Jesus take away sin, he destroyed it. Our sins are not covered by the blood of Jesus, they were *taken away* to be remembered no more by God. It didn't happen when you started trying to live an acceptably moral lifestyle, or when you were baptized in water. Confirmation, communion, dedication, and rededication had nothing to do with it. *Nada.* It occurred at the one-time sacrifice of Jesus Christ because of God's love for you, and this has been made available to the entire world. The completed act for our forgiveness will do us no good if we're still spiritually dead. The work Christ did to bring us redemption and forgiveness has already occurred, yet we receive and experience the reality of this blessing in a personal way through belief. Simply trust that his finished work was sufficient and that there is nothing we can add to it.

Don't read any further until you answer this crucial question out loud. *Was Jesus successful in what he came to do, or was he a failure?* Your answer will determine what you choose to believe about God's forgiveness. Are you able to trust that he did enough to get the job done, or are you going to try to add something in order to finish what he started, but didn't complete?

"You know that he appeared in order to take away sins, and in him there is no sin" (1 John 3:5).

Did you catch that? He came to take away sins. In him there is no sin. As a believer in Jesus Christ, you are in him. Connect the dots.

(12) THE SIN CONFESSION OBSESSION

IT CAN BE SO EASY TO LOSE OUR PERIPHERAL VISION when we are caught building a particular doctrine around an individual verse from the Bible. Spiritual tunnel vision will cause blind spots that result in losing our awareness of a more complete truth that surrounds us. I'm about to address a subject that the religious establishment relentlessly hammers into believers, and they will become visibly and verbally upset whenever this ideology is challenged. That subject is the ongoing confession of individual sins.

My intent is not to discourage confession entirely, but if your main purpose in doing so is to receive a renewed forgiveness from God, then I would not encourage that. Crying out to God for forgiveness under the former covenant was constantly ongoing because of the many sacrifices bringing a guilty conscience or reminder of sin. But as the foregoing chapter clearly explained, the act of forgiveness from God for the sins of the world was dealt with at the cross, because Jesus came to destroy and take away sin.

Unnecessary Confession

A noteworthy truth to consider is that the apostle who wrote more books of the New Testament than anyone else never exhorted us to confess our sins to be forgiven. You would think if confession of all your sins were a requirement in order to receive forgiveness, Paul would've mentioned this over and over and expounded upon it further. After all, this would've been a pretty big deal.

When the Philippian jailer fell down before Paul and asked what he needed to do to be saved, Paul didn't say to ask God for forgiveness. He said to believe on the Lord Jesus. From the start of his conversion, he wasn't instructed to ask God to forgive him, so why would he need to do it thereafter? This is just something that has been added to the booklet of religious rules. To be saved means to heal, preserve and rescue (Strong's G4982). Some word studies show this is primarily used as God rescuing people from the penalty and power of sin, and delivering them into safety. *He* is your refuge.

A common mindset found within empty religion is that God will forgive you no matter how many times you ask him. Scripture has even better news for us! There is a reason why you won't find the phrase "ask God for forgiveness" anywhere in the New Testament. It's because forgiveness was based upon blood that has already been shed—not because of any work on our part—and that includes confession of one's individual sins. In my journey, I believe it was somewhere around confession number 6,666 where I just wore out. I was so busy trying to stay clean and forgiven, I couldn't hear the Spirit of God compassionately shouting at me to stop. When we begin to realize our sins far exceed our confessions, there is nowhere else to turn except to trust in the blood of Jesus Christ and his finished work.

It should be pointed out the apostles did not have differing views about confession and forgiveness, as Peter confirms in Acts 10:43, "To him all the prophets bear witness that everyone who believes in him receives forgiveness of sins through his name." So which is it? Forgiveness by believing in the work of Jesus or the conditional requirement of repeated confessions of sin? Covenant clashers will say it's both, but this is the result of combining the old and new covenants together. It can't be both, otherwise we would have to depend on *ourselves* and be responsible for confessing each individual sin to ensure we'll be forgiven. This wrongly puts you and I back on center stage and weakens the message of the infallible cross. At the risk of being repetitive, it's really quite simple—the work of forgiveness was completed at the cross, but we receive this gift by believing.

It's time to take a breath now and ask ourselves a question: *As believers in Christ, why would we want to continue seeking forgiveness that has already been provided, by confessing sins under a better covenant where God says he remembers them no more, no longer counts them against us, and isn't dealing with us according to our sins?*

Considering that God has already done all he is going to do about forgiveness through the cross of Christ, where do we get this idea about the need for ongoing confession of all our sins in order to be forgiven? As we go to the source, we discover it pretty much revolves around one individual verse in the entire Bible found in 1 John 1:9. There are eight verses leading up to that confession verse in the first chapter from John's letter; therefore our awareness of the context is vital to understanding what is being stated when it comes to the issue of confession. His opening statement is making the case that Jesus absolutely came to earth as a man, so let's jump into it with John's introduction:

> "That which was from the beginning, which we have heard, which we have seen with our eyes, which we looked upon and have touched with our hands, concerning the word of life—the life was made manifest, and we have seen it, and testify to it and proclaim to you the eternal life, which was with the Father and was made manifest to us—that which we have seen and heard we proclaim also to you, so that you too may have fellowship with us; and indeed our fellowship is with the Father and with his Son Jesus Christ. And we are writing these things so that our joy may be complete" (1 John 1:1-4).

The key words here are *looked upon, touched, seen,* and *heard.* Why? There are legitimate questions raised by students of Scripture as to who John was actually speaking to at the beginning of his letter. Many think he was addressing Gnostics, and while I don't pretend to be an expert on this group, there is much to be found when studying this movement, and you may even find notes on them within your study Bible. Historians have identified that certain Gnostic sects did not believe Jesus came in the flesh because they were persuaded God would never stoop so low as to become human. They might have argued any so-called appearance of the Son of God was an illusion performed with smoke and mirrors, so to speak. They did not recognize the outward appearing of Jesus as a man or the fact that sin even existed.

As a rule, the presumption among Christians is that all Scripture in the New Testament is written only to address believers. However, as we look carefully throughout this first chapter, we'll see that John begins the letter by writing to these unbelieving people who were embedded with believers in that community—people who had not yet come to faith or a belief in Christ. This is why he hits the ground running by starting out with the testimony that he and others had seen (Christ) with their eyes, touched him with their hands, heard him with their ears, and saw the manifestation of eternal life in human form. In fact, in order to get his point across, the above passage has John stating four different times that he and others had seen and looked at Jesus. John is speaking to people who were of the persuasion that Jesus was not born of a woman, and he is proclaiming the message of the gospel with whom he longs to have fellowship with, because as of now, they are not in fellowship with each other. He does not have a joy that is complete regarding them. John continues:

> "This is the message we have heard from him and proclaim to you, that God is light, and in him is no darkness at all. If we say we have fellowship with him while we walk in darkness, we lie and do not practice the truth. But if we walk in the light, as he is in the light, we have fellowship with one another, and the blood of Jesus his Son cleanses us from all sin" (1 John 1:5-7).

What does it mean to walk in darkness? To deny Christ is to deny God; you can't have the Father without the Son. Those who believe in Christ are in the light; there is no darkness in him at all. As children of the light, we have fellowship with each other because of our common fellowship with the Lord. If you can walk in and out of spiritual darkness based on your performance and behavior, then the blood of Jesus Christ would have to be considered inadequate. Scripture declares his finished work was more than enough (with blood that cleanses us from *all* sin), thus we should avoid biting on the bait from the enemy that would lead us into covenant confusion by thinking forgiveness has suddenly become based on certain conditions.

The next three verses (8–10) are the primary focus of those teaching that Christians need to confess their sins to stay forgiven. Let's zip through these verses one after the other, keeping in mind the context discussed above. Here in verse 8, John continues to address these unbelievers with whom he longs to have fellowship with, and who say there is no sin: "If we say we have no sin, we deceive ourselves, and the truth is not in us" (1 John 1:8).

Verse 9 is the one that is frequently quoted and gets all the attention about confession: "If we confess our sins, he is faithful and just to forgive us our sins and to cleanse us from all unrighteousness" (1 John 1:9).

Finally, in verse 10, John is still talking to the same group as when he started the chapter: "If we say we have not sinned, we make him a liar, and his word is not in us" (1 John 1:10).

The word *sin* and *sins* in our English language is generally translated from two Greek words: *hamartia* is a noun, which usually indicates a *sin condition* that was found in us through Adam (Strong's G266). The other Greek word is *hamartano*, and it is a verb that would refer more to specific sinful actions (Strong's G264). Both words are defined very similarly, which means "to miss the mark." Simply put, the primary difference for humankind is that the noun led to the verb. In fact, it's interesting to note that the noun for the word sin (or sins) appears nearly four times more often than the verb in the New Testament. The difference between a sin condition and sinful actions can be significant, especially in the context of confession.

In verses 7 to 9, we find the noun is used when referring to sin and sins, but in verse 10, the word "sinned" is the verb. Therefore, we admit and agree there had been a sin problem, and that all have sinned. Those who deny it are making God out to be a liar and we know it is impossible for God to lie. In fact, to confess means to acknowledge or agree.

You see, John is urging unbelieving people to confess (acknowledge) the sin condition, and that they've sinned, thereby leading them to an admission of needing a savior. He is *not* suggesting that Christians confess every single sin in order to be forgiven all over again, as though the blood of Jesus had limited powers. We're in a new and *better* covenant, and there is no fine print or legal addendum within this agreement that states "you are hereby forgiven for sin, unless you commit another sin." To be openly blunt, it's absolutely kooky that covenant clashers have injected this doctrine into the Christian mindset. Talk about a blueprint for bondage!

Continuing on the issue of the sin condition and sinful actions, the Apostle Paul addressed this as well:

> "Therefore, just as sin came into the world through one man, and death through sin, and so death spread to all men because all sinned—for sin indeed was in the world before the law was given, but sin is not counted where there is no law" (Romans 5:12-13).

Death came to the human race through the sin condition (noun) inherited from Adam, and it spread to everyone because all have sinned (verb). When the law came into play, sin was counted against people, or charged to their account. In a New Covenant where the law has been brought to an end and put aside, God no longer counts trespasses against us.

Some might wonder what type of sin God has taken away through the sacrifice of Christ. Is it the sin condition or the sinful actions? We can be thankful it is all forms of sin that he conquered and destroyed in order to cleanse us from all unrighteousness. This includes a sinful nature, as well as sinful actions, making us free from a sin consciousness—a freedom which could not be found in a system filled with animal sacrifices.

When it comes to the Word of God declaring that sin has been taken away, it's obviously not describing the outward *manifestation* of sin found in behavioral choices. But in a new and better covenant where Christ demonstrated perfect love towards us, God turned off the scoreboard and is not keeping a record of wrong. Think about that the next time you're singing the old hymn of "Power in the Blood." Although many in the church will ponder whether it sounds too good to be true, we're talking about a wonder-working power that will free you from the burden of sin.

The sooner we come to grips with this, the more likely we'll begin to see supernatural, victorious choices manifesting in our lives.

* * *

Because it has been erroneously assumed by many that John is addressing believers in his first chapter, covenant clashers will argue that since John used the words *us* and *we*, he is referring to "us Christians." But the context we covered leading up to this—along with what is to follow—should bring us to the conclusion that John's reference is to people in general (human beings). Christian believers would not have denied they've sinned. They would have previously acknowledged they had sinned, and confessed their need for a Savior. It's another reason why we know John's target audience in this chapter wasn't believers, but a group of people blinded to the truth of Jesus Christ who were in a community of believers. Any local church body may have a mixture of Christians who have trusted Christ, and those who haven't yet come to the saving knowledge of his grace. This likely would've been magnified in the culture of the early church.

John would begin to engage believers after this first chapter, as evidenced by the fact that his language changes when he speaks about them having an anointing from the holy one and begins addressing his children, a term used by a teacher to their disciples (students). In fact, to begin the second chapter of this letter, he exhorts them to avoid the act of sinning, but if anyone does sin, we always have an advocate with the Father—Jesus Christ the righteous. John follows by dropping this bombshell: "He is the propitiation for our sins, and not for ours only but also for the sins of the whole world" (1 John 2:2). *The sins of the whole world!*

There is a theme going forward throughout this letter, as John will continuously remind believers that Jesus Christ arrived among people, and brought eternal life:

> "I write to you, not because you do not know the truth, but because you know it, and because no lie is of the truth. Who is the liar but he who denies that Jesus is the Christ? This is the

antichrist, he who denies the Father and the Son. No one who denies the Son has the Father. Whoever confesses the Son has the Father also. I write these things to you about those who are trying to deceive you" (1 John 2:21-23, 26).

Considering the context that has been addressed from the first chapter, John just revealed a big reason for the purpose of this letter in chapter two: *I'm writing so you won't be deceived by others who are delivering a message that is against Christ. You can't have the Father without confessing the Son!* As we step back from the trees for a better view of the forest, we can clearly see the difference from when John is talking to believers who know the truth, compared to the first chapter of his letter, when he was addressing people who were deceiving themselves, and "did not have the truth in them."

Later in his letter, observe how John will exhort believers by going back to the subject of "confessing" the truth of Christ coming to earth as a man: "By this you know the Spirit of God: every spirit that confesses that Jesus Christ has come in the flesh is from God" (1 John 4:2).

Again, towards the very end of the letter, John clarifies he is now writing to believers by reminding them about Christ coming as a man:

> "I write these things to you who believe in the name of the Son of God that you may know that you have eternal life. And we know that the Son of God has come and has given us understanding, so that we may know him who is true; and we are in him who is true, in his Son Jesus Christ. He is the true God and eternal life" (1 John 5:13, 20).

Once again in his next letter he writes: "For many deceivers have gone out into the world, those who do not confess the coming of Jesus Christ in the flesh. Such a one is the deceiver and the antichrist" (2 John 1:7).

One Sacrifice, One Confession

Whenever the Israelites fell short and sinned, more sacrifices were performed and they would try again and again with the same failed results. This was the curse of the law they were under—the requirement to follow all of the commandments perfectly, but having the inability to do it. Does this seem similar to what you've gone through in your own life? Religion has attempted to use confession of sins as a new covenant alternative for animal sacrifices. In other words, covenant clashers have reasoned since Christ was only sacrificed once, the burden of sin confession would fall upon us to be used as a substitute for blood in order to keep the forgiveness faucet turned on. This is why we must recognize the plenitude of forgiveness that came through the cross. There is no forgiveness without blood, yet it was only needed once with Christ.

Unfortunately, the ongoing confession obsession takes people down the same path the Jews were traveling before the cross, bringing a consciousness of sin from which they couldn't escape. Although it may be done out of ignorance and a lack of understanding, confessing to gain renewed forgiveness is the result of not realizing the sufficiency of Christ's one sacrifice. Jesus said his yoke was easy and his burden was light. This does not describe the burden of trying to confess every wrong thought and action. Just as there was one sacrifice needed to establish the New Covenant, there is one confession for salvation within this covenant, and it is a confession of the Lord Jesus Christ:

> "... that if you confess with your mouth Jesus as Lord, and believe in your heart that God raised Him from the dead, you will be saved; for with the heart a person believes, resulting in righteousness, and with the mouth he confesses, resulting in salvation. For the Scripture says, 'Whoever believes in Him will not be disappointed.' For there is no distinction between Jew and Greek; for the same Lord is Lord of all, abounding in riches for all who call on Him; for 'Whoever will call upon the name of the Lord will be saved' " (Romans 10:9-13 NASB).

This is a crucial moment to do some serious dot connecting. Paul just declared that when one believes, it results in righteousness, while confessing Jesus Christ as Lord would result in salvation. Now rewind to when John was on the same subject of confession; he stated it would result in God cleansing us from *all* unrighteousness. A believer in Christ has not been gifted with a new heart containing both righteousness and unrighteousness from within. We don't have to keep taking a spiritual bath in order to scrub off what has already been cleansed by the blood of Jesus, once and for all. Although John and Paul wrote different books to different people, they are both on the same page in referring to a confession or acknowledgement of sin, thereby leading to one confession or acknowledgement of the Lord Jesus. This brings salvation, coinciding with belief that leads to an eternal righteousness.

While religion continues to advertise 1 John 1:9 out of context on billboards for Christians, here is something John stated later in the same letter that is often overlooked: "Whoever confesses that Jesus is the Son of God, God abides in him, and he in God" (1 John 4:15). That doesn't sound to me as though fellowship with the Lord will wane or weaken based on our paltry efforts or maintaining a constant confession of sin. What we see here is John revealing the true intent of how he started off the letter in the first chapter—the confession of Jesus Christ, leading to salvation, abiding in intimate fellowship with him and with one another.

Along with what Paul stated in the tenth chapter of Romans, he also related the same thing to Timothy in regards to the one confession that leads to the salvation of eternal life: "Fight the good fight of the faith. Take hold of the eternal life to which you were called and about which you made the good confession in the presence of many witnesses" (1 Timothy 6:12).

This is the kind of confession John was talking about in his letter, a confession of Christ for unbelievers to receive the gift of salvation. Unlike the Gnostics, in order to believe God raised Jesus from the dead, naturally one would also believe Jesus came in the flesh, in human form. As believers, our *ongoing* confession isn't meant to be focused on our sinful failures that God remembers no more. Our confession is now rooted in who Jesus is and belief in what he has done.

It is not my intention to be overly dogmatic on the theory that John started out the letter writing to those of the Gnostic persuasion. The point being made is that in the first chapter of 1 John, he wasn't writing to believers in Christ, nor does it appear he was writing to those of the Jewish faith, who were still clinging to the law. Both Christians and Jews would not be part of a belief system that states "we have no sin." Again,

Christians would have acknowledged the need for a savior because of a sin problem. Likewise, through the law and animal sacrifices, Jews also recognized sin existed.

A Sin Condition

The entire passage from the first chapter of 1 John is more evangelistic in nature, targeting those who haven't yet come to recognize the sinful condition they were born into through Adam. This condition (noun) was an even bigger problem than sinful actions (verb), because through Adam's one offense, we inherited the condition that resulted in condemnation and led to the manifestation of sin in our lives.

This may cause one to say, "Golly, that doesn't seem fair! We didn't do anything wrong before being pronounced guilty!" In contrast to this, the last Adam (Jesus) came along, and through his righteous act, life was made freely available to those who would receive the abundance of grace. We entered into righteousness without having done anything to deserve it. That doesn't seem fair either, right? Just ask the older son from the prodigal parable.

Judgment arose from Adam's *one* transgression and resulted in condemnation, and this brought a guilty verdict to all. On the other hand, the one righteous act by Jesus delivered the free gift which arose from *many* transgressions, resulting in justification. This brought a verdict with a declaration of innocence. A "legal" precedent had been established—all were declared guilty in Adam, so the gift of righteousness could be made available to all through Jesus Christ, as Paul describes:

> "Therefore, as one trespass led to condemnation for all men, so one act of righteousness leads to justification and life for all men. For as by the one man's disobedience [Adam] the many were made sinners, so by the one man's obedience [Jesus] the many will be made righteous" (Romans 5:18-19) *Brackets added.*

For even more context, back up a few chapters in Romans and follow all the way through to what Paul says here when referring to *all men*, meaning that justification and life would not be limited to the nation of Israel. He specifies reference to not only Jews, but Gentiles as well. We find in these passages from Romans that the people of Israel were also guilty and had fallen short. Their covenant with God did not place them in a position of favor when it came to the righteousness of God. It was not only those unclean Gentiles who were declared sinners, but *all men*, or all races of people, Jew and Gentile, whether they were under the law or not. This inheritance of righteousness would not be by the law of works, but by faith or belief as it was with Abraham through the promise. Contrary to the message of fear coming from many pulpits today, we have obtained "an inheritance that is imperishable, undefiled, and unfading" (1 Peter 1:3–4).

To put this another way, we needed one single sacrifice that would permanently address the "verbs," referring to every single, sinful action that would ever occur in our lives. Why? Because we're still living in a fallen world with corrupt bodies that haven't been redeemed yet, and we can never perform enough penance or do anything on our own to ensure we have attained forgiveness for every wrongful thought or deed. Here in the New Covenant, the issue is more about the "noun," referring to the condition of the heart that brings either condemnation through unbelief, or a state of righteousness by believing (see John 3:18).

Prior to the cross, the sinful nature and sinful actions would sometimes go together like peas and carrots, leading to a "domino effect." In the New Covenant, believers "in Christ" no longer have a wicked heart and are not defined as sinners, but rather as saints. The very root of the sin problem (within our spirits) has been remedied by the cross.

Although the Greek noun for "sin" doesn't necessarily mean a specific reference to a "sinful condition" by itself in every instance it appears, think of it in this way: A sinful condition of the heart triggered sinful actions. However, sinful actions do not cause a sinful heart. The same is true for a new heart or condition of righteousness; it can generate righteous acts, but performing works of righteousness is not what brings us a righteous condition. Listen, we should seek to avoid committing sin because it's a bad thing and hurts people in multiple ways, but sin is no longer the obstacle keeping anyone from becoming children and heirs of God, according to the promise, as Paul shares with Titus:

"But when the goodness and loving kindness of God our Savior appeared, he saved us, not because of works done by us in righteousness, but according to his own mercy, by the washing of regeneration and renewal of the Holy Spirit, whom he poured out on us richly through Jesus Christ our Savior, so that being justified by his grace we might become heirs according to the hope of eternal life" (Titus 4-7).

Paul continued by exhorting believers to devote themselves to good works. But the gift of righteousness and a new nature that is born of God within the heart ... this is received by believing in the name of Jesus Christ (see John 1:12-13).

The world of religion has had an unhealthy obsession with a sin consciousness, and rarely do they ever communicate the truth as it relates to believers becoming the righteousness of God. This is where the focus should be! It wouldn't matter whether you had one sin or one million sins that were unforgiven, because neither would be acceptable before a holy God. Forgiveness means "to send away, release" (Strong's G863). On the issue of forgiveness, those nasty verbs—the sinful actions of the entire world—were dealt with by God putting them away for all time through Christ at the cross. Get ready for a rerun that was previously stated: If this is not the way things are, Jesus would have to keep suffering with repeated sacrifices, as the high priests had to do under the law. Thankfully, our High Priest has no need for any of that.

The Confession Math Doesn't Add Up

Along with the lack of instruction or exhortation in the Scriptures about sin confession, common sense should tell us that confession of individual sins is not required to be forgiven. For one thing, you won't be able to confess them all. You'll miss something, and I can guarantee you'll do it on a regular basis. And what about those poor souls over many centuries that had never been exposed to such a verse and had all those unconfessed sins? We forget that Bibles were not being spit out of a printing press in those days for all the world to comb through.

So what would happen if we *really* needed to confess them all to be forgiven? The truth is, we would be doomed. The math just wouldn't add up because it's fuzzy math. But covenant clashers think they have that all worked out. They'll instruct you to simply do what I call the "blanket confession" to cover everything that you couldn't specifically manage to get confessed.

I must confess here that the blanket prayer was one I fell back on pretty regularly during the dreary days of my covenant confusion. This is where you ask to be forgiven for everything all over again including the things you don't know or don't remember. Whew! Doesn't that make you feel better? If it does, I assure you it's only temporary before you'll end up right back at square one. Not to mention that you're about to enter a new hour and soon another day, then a week ... and if you don't keep up with every wrong thought and action without confessing, the needle on the sin meter will be spinning like a fan. So the cycle continues. As those who were under the former covenant would've told you, this reminder of sin just leads to more sinning and more guilt.

If you're going to take a single verse of Scripture out of context and make a case for it—referring to individual actions of sin that require repeated confessions to maintain forgiveness—the blanket approach isn't valid because you're not specifically confessing all of them. Inevitably, you may start to wonder if the blanket confession will be enough.

When you begin feeling too guilty or unworthy, religion will soon have you reaching for the heavy artillery; yes, that's right—the dreaded *rededication prayer.* If the burden of guilt is *still* too overwhelming, it might even mean responding to the invitation for the rededication prayer at the front of the church at a place often nicknamed the "altar." The altar is an old covenant position, and though you may walk away feeling pretty good emotionally, you'll probably end up back there again just like those in Israel kept doing. The spiritual ego you'll feel from rededicating your life to God will just be "altar ego" that is temporary and feeds on self-righteousness. In some church denominations, it may be another variation of ceremonial "insurance" that one may feel is needed, such as another round of water baptism.

So even after hundreds and thousands of confessions and recommitments, you'll still be wondering where you stand with God in any given hour, week, or month. How many sins got missed this time and is my slate *really* clean? Can you see the problem with this? Does this sound like good news? If you think the tax code is complicated, just wait until the religious code is applied and someone from the ERS (External Religious Service) comes around to collect. They'll audit your records while searching for wrongdoing and will demand accountability for every mistake they can find (or that you'll confess). No matter how much you pay, you'll never be debt-free, because the ERS will always demand more.

It's natural to feel sorry about missing the mark and for poor choices we make, but misguided thinking that sorrow and apologies will bring a renewed forgiveness from God is only in our minds. Confession of sins in order to be forgiven is really more about you being able to forgive yourself, and this will be better accomplished by understanding that God isn't relating to you according to your failures, but through Christ, where he has placed you.

Confessing sins to be forgiven is like being on a nutritional diet. You'll get so focused on avoiding bad food that all you can think about is having what you're trying to avoid. What happens when you blow it and dive into the "sin" of candy or ice cream? Frustration and guilt for giving in will often cause shame and lead to avoiding the scale of accountability. People will reason within themselves that since they failed, why not partake of more junk for awhile and start over again later with a renewed commitment to try harder the next time. But they end up with the same results. We should never be afraid of the accountability scale. Even if you were to put every single sin on it that you have ever committed, the shed blood of Jesus Christ would always tilt the scale in your favor.

I've been through the constant battle of trying to stay forgiven through confession of sins. Sometimes it wasn't so much that I felt the guilt of doing the wrong things, but I found myself struggling with the sense that I wasn't doing enough of the right things. I would often deem myself alienated from God, based on my performance. Over time, it would accumulate to where I would reach the end of an overwhelmed emotional cycle and feel the need to rededicate my life and start over with a clean slate and second chance. But I've learned that second chances aren't always as great as they are advertised to be.

When we talk about God giving us second chances, it implies that our right standing with him is contingent upon our behavior or performance. This wrongfully places the responsibility on us instead of Jesus Christ. The Old Covenant was known for second chances with one animal sacrifice after the other. I wish I had discovered earlier in life that I didn't need a second chance, and that my slate was already clean. From my perspective, it was as if my account had been overdrawn, and in my mind I wasn't sure where I stood with God. *No believer in Christ should ever feel that way.* The life we have in him is more than a feeling, and it's one that brings peace of mind, so don't look back.

> "And you, who once were alienated and enemies *in your mind* by wicked works, yet now He has reconciled in the body of His flesh through death, to present you holy, and blameless, and above reproach in His sight—if indeed you continue in the faith, grounded and steadfast, and are not moved away from the hope of the gospel which you heard, which was preached to every creature under heaven, of which I, Paul, became a minister" (Colossians 1:21–23 NKJV). *Italics added.*

It's incredible for us to have been presented by Jesus as holy and blameless before God. I can hear the doubters saying, "Yes, but it's based on the condition that we continue in the faith!" Frequently our idea of faith wrongly revolves around doing, coupled with performance in the framework of lifestyle choices. Faith is a foundation upon which other things are built, one that brings us a conviction, evidence, or proof of things we don't always see but which can be manifested. Faith is not a condition or work on our part, but *a gift* from the Lord (see Ephesians 2:8). It is simply a *response* from our heart. It is the very *substance* of what we hope for (Christ), and I believe our understanding of this gift will increase as we grow in grace while having our minds renewed. Continuing in the faith is simply trusting in what *Jesus did* by unconditionally presenting us as righteous, holy, and blameless. We should seek to continue abiding in the faith of Christ's finished work, not our own unfinished effort.

Believers under the Old Covenant died in faith and were commended through their faith, but in spite of all the great manifestations or even persecutions they experienced, they did not receive what was promised under that covenant (see Hebrews 11:13, 39). Think about that—we have received what those old covenant giants of the faith could not.

Unhindered Fellowship

Some ministers in the land of the legal will argue that ongoing sin and a lack of sin confession will cause a type of relationship separation, and they will insist specific sins that are not confessed will hinder your fellowship with God. I used to think this way too. I was wrong. Fellowship with God is cloaked in our union with Christ. Regardless of how our failures may make us feel (bad at first), it doesn't change God's perspective of us.

Here's another Chapter 1, verse 9 Scripture that would be profitable for us to remember from 1 Corinthians: "God is faithful, by whom you were called into the fellowship of his Son, Jesus Christ our Lord."

God is faithful even when we are not (see 2 Timothy 2:13). He *called* you into fellowship, and he isn't going to recall his callings. He isn't going to change his mind and turn his back on you, avoid you, ignore you, or anything else that would interrupt that relationship with you. Hey, you can go to church and get that kind of treatment from your fellow inmates. We're not new and improved, but new and *approved.*

Since our fellowship with God is always ongoing for us now, you can stop wondering from time to time if God has left the house in anger, and whether he will be knocking on the door so you can invite him back. He isn't going anywhere! Besides, we were invited into *his* household as a bona fide member of the family, not as a tenant with the potential for eviction. When one wrongfully fears they have lost fellowship with God, they will lose the desire to fellowship with others and miss the blessing of relationships.

Although confession isn't a requirement, there may be times where there is a place for it, but not for the purpose of seeking forgiveness. Sometimes we just feel the need or have the desire to approach the throne of grace. It's okay to unload on God. It can be good for the soul and provide an emotional release. But we should do it with intimacy and confidence, not crawling on our stomach with feelings of unworthiness, begging for forgiveness (see Hebrews 4:14-16). That would be an insult to the finished work of Christ. If you feel the need for affirmation of mercy or to find grace to help in time of need, God has plenty to go around, so allow him to reassure you.

Perhaps you need to talk with someone and release some things you've bottled up. James said to "confess your sins to one another and pray for one another" (James 5:16). He didn't say this would be for the purpose of acquiring forgiveness, but it can bring emotional healing. A word of caution: be careful not to spill intimate information to someone who has a need to confess that they have a struggle with gossip. This is also known as "the gift of sharing." (*"I'm only telling you this so you can pray for so and so."*) We've already learned what that will result into since humans love a good secret, whether it's leaking one or just being all ears.

Our preoccupation shouldn't be with sin, but with the person of Jesus Christ and the accomplishment of his finished work. If you find yourself "doing" (or not doing) something in an attempt to establish right standing with God, you've crossed over into fleshly minded territory. Others who are in this religious quicksand will try to drag you down with them because misery loves company, as Paul explains in Colossians 2:18, 20-23 (NKJV):

> "Let no one cheat you of your reward, taking delight in false humility and worship of angels, intruding into those things which he has not seen, vainly puffed up by his fleshly mind.
>
> "Therefore, if you died with Christ from the basic principles of the world, why, as though living in the world, do you subject yourselves to regulations—'Do not touch, do not taste, do not handle,' which all concern things which perish with the using—according to the commandments and doctrines of men? These things indeed have an appearance of wisdom in self-imposed religion, false humility, and neglect of the body, but are of no value against the indulgence of the flesh."

God has rewarded you with the guarantee of grace in the person of Jesus Christ. Believe it, and don't let those controlling religious principalities and powers defraud you of it. In the New Covenant, you are not defined as a "sinner saved by grace." While sin may still occur outwardly and you have been saved by grace, you are now considered a saint, a part of the family, and a member of the household of God. Those who continue to spiritually identify themselves as sinners will likely keep struggling, while frequently yielding to poor choices. They stay imprisoned within a mindset that assumes they are "just a sinner," where overcoming on a regular basis seems more like science fiction than reality. Never forget that your identity in him is based upon what Christ did at the cross on our behalf. Here are just a few examples of how God identifies you as a believer in Christ. Again, to confess means to agree, and these ought to be part of your confession from this day forward:

- You are alive (Galatians 2:20; Ephesians 2:5).
- You are anointed (2 Corinthians 1:21–22; 1 John 2:20, 27).
- You are blameless (1 Corinthians 1:8; Ephesians 1:4; Colossians 1:22)
- You are complete (Colossians 2:10).
- You are forgiven (Colossians 1:14, 2:13-14; Ephesians 1:7; 1 John 2:12).
- You are holy (1 Corinthians 3:17; Ephesians 5:27; Colossians 3:12; Hebrews 3:1).
- You have peace (John 14:27; Romans 5:1-2a; Ephesians 2:14; Philippians 4:7).
- You are perfected (Hebrews 10:14; 1 Peter 5:10).
- You are reconciled (Romans 5:10; 2 Corinthians 5:18-19; Colossians 1:22).
- You are righteous (Titus 3:4-7; 2 Corinthians 5:21; Romans 1:17; Romans 3:21).
- You are sanctified (1 Corinthians 1:30, 6:11; Hebrews 10:10, 14).

The sin confession conclusion: The cross of Jesus Christ was not a failed experiment. There is no Plan B, nor is there the need for one. Confession of each sin to seek forgiveness is the equivalent of performing old covenant animal sacrifices ... the burden to follow through will be upon you and you'll never be able to keep up.

You might not know it from the sermons you've heard over the years, but sin is *not* stronger than the mighty power of the blood of the lamb of God. In this covenant, sin cannot bring a separation because it was removed, destroyed, taken away and remembered no more. When one lacks understanding of the finished work of the cross, there will be multiple, ongoing, repeated confessions of sin, resulting in sorrow. However, realizing that his blood is eternally stronger than sin will lead to a confession of Christ, resulting in peace. He died only once, and he did it for all.

(13) CURSE FREE (UNLESS YOU DON'T TITHE?)

R ELIGION WILL PERSISTENTLY ATTEMPT to make it appear as though Gentiles are meant to be under law. If it's not the Mosaic law, it will be a modernized version of it. Much like there were many hundreds of laws or commands in a package called *the law*, the same is true with the many curses mentioned in the Old Covenant contained in what would be called *the curse*, arriving through that same law.

To give you an idea of comparing the old curse to the new blessing in Christ, the Old Testament had approximately one-hundred-seventy (170) references with the words *curse*, *curses*, or *cursed* in the NASB version. Compare that to about thirteen (13) listed in the pages of the New Testament, none of which refer to us being under a curse or imply that we are being cursed in any way. This is just a simplistic approach to illustrate the many curses that came through the law compared to none found in the covenant of grace.

Here are samples of just a few dishes still being served to Christians from the previous and now obsolete menu:

• **Deuteronomy 11:26-28:** "See, I am setting before you today a blessing and a curse: the blessing, if you obey the commandments of the LORD your God, which I command you today, and the curse, if you do not obey the commandments of the LORD your God, but turn aside from the way that I am commanding you today, to go after other gods that you have not known."

• **Deuteronomy 27:26:** "Cursed is the one who does not confirm the words of this law by doing them. And all the people shall say, 'Amen!' "

• **Joshua 1:8:** "This book of the law shall not depart from your mouth, but you shall meditate on it day and night, so that you may be careful to do according to all that is written in it; for then you will make your way prosperous, and then you will have success."

Without the knowledge that there are two distinct and different covenants, one might assume the above passages would apply to us today. Under the Old, if you followed all the commands of the law, you would be blessed, find success, and make your way prosperous. On the flip side, fail once and you'd be cursed. The bad news is that everybody failed under that covenant. If you've spent money on a Christian success seminar and that verse from Joshua was touted as the infrastructure for your prosperity, I would ask for a refund.

To be specific, the curse of the law required following all of it perfectly, while having the inability to accomplish it. Remember, Paul's message of good news in Galatians 3:13 for the Jews was that Christ came to redeem them from this curse of the law by becoming a curse for the people.

The Tithing Curse

You'll still find people warning about the danger of falling under curses from the law that Israel has been freed from. Which begs the question— why would we Gentiles be considered under a curse that was contained in an obsolete covenant which we were never invited into in the first place?

Church attendees from many denominations have most likely heard a good deal of teaching about a curse related to the issue of tithing. There are plenty of books available on the subject of the tithe, both pro and con. Those who are teaching that tithing should be an application for our lives under the New Covenant will bend over backwards to blot out the jots and fiddle with the tittles in order to rearrange the dots of the bigger picture. But the pixels in the image they present lacks resolution. Pay special attention and I believe you'll see most of those dots are out of order and just don't fit in the covenant that we are now under. It's a hotly debated topic, and people can easily walk away confused—and when there is confusion, you'll often find an attempt to mix portions of the two covenants together.

The subject of giving under the New Covenant is addressed in the next chapter, but I want to go over a few basic points about tithing first, because there are far too many people who think they are cursed for not having tithed on a regular basis, and this is no way to go through life. I've heard ridiculous messages from pulpits warning of the danger of hell for not giving ten percent of all your income, so here's some prose and perspective on this topic from Malachi 3:8-10 (NKJV):

> "Will a man rob God?
> Yet you have robbed Me!
> But you say, 'In what way have we robbed You?'
> In tithes and offerings.
> You are cursed with a curse,
> For you have robbed Me,
> Even this whole nation.
> Bring all the tithes into the storehouse,
> That there may be food in My house,
> And try Me now in this,"
> Says the Lord of hosts,
> "If I will not open for you the windows of heaven
> And pour out for you such blessing
> That there will not be room enough to receive it."

Notice the plural of the word *tithes*. Quite often it is assumed they are called tithes because they are something being collected from multiple people. But the reason for the plural is because there were different types of tithes, and they were used for different purposes under the law.

Although Malachi is almost always the go-to passage today for teaching people to tithe, it is the *last* reference on the subject in the Old Testament. This is not an instruction on how to tithe because there were already many other Scriptures under the law explaining the rules of tithing to the Jewish people. Due to incompatibility issues with the covenants, it would be quite rare for most churches to teach about tithing from the Old Testament prior to Malachi, but the law has much to say about the subject, and can be found in places such as Leviticus, Numbers, Deuteronomy, 2 Chronicles, Nehemiah, and Amos. It would be helpful to go to those earlier books and *work your way forward* to find out what tithes really were, and why it led them to being mentioned in Malachi.

A tithe simply means one-tenth; to set aside one-tenth of something (Strong's H4643). It does *not* mean to give ten percent of all your income or everything you have. Tithes had virtually nothing to do with money, and Israel was never instructed to tithe of its money. Of course, Israelites would earn and spend money, and they had purchased possessions they enjoyed. They probably also used money to give to others, but they were not commanded to tithe of their money. However, as we'll see, they could turn their tithe into money.

There were twelve tribes in Israel, plus the Levites, which was the priestly tribe. Not all Levites were priests, but they were a part of the tribe that served in the priesthood. When the nation inherited the Promised Land, Levites did not inherit land or cattle as the other tribes did, and they were forbidden to work in the fields. Instead, their inheritance would be tithes from the other tribes. In turn, they would provide the ministry of the priesthood for the rest of the tribes of Israel. Included with their inheritance would be cities for the Levites to dwell in and small pasturelands around those cities for livestock. Therefore, the main purpose for tithing was so the Levites would be fed by the other tribes.

In reality, the other tribes were not sacrificing anything, and this was completely fair. Why? The amount of their land and harvest would have been less if the Levites had been given the same inheritance. Basically, the other tribes were providing what would have already belonged to the Levites if God had not designated that tribe to the work of the priesthood. This is vastly different from the money related to "church tithing" that is taught today.

In order to get a general description of how tithes worked, you can read for yourself in Deuteronomy 14:22-29 and also in Deuteronomy 26:10-13. Here is a summary: The Israelites would tithe from the increase of their *food.* They would share their tithe with the Levites at a place designated by God. If they were unable to carry their tithes, or if the place to travel was too far away, they could exchange their tithe for money. They would take the money to the chosen place and spend it "on whatever their hearts desired," and they would eat there before God. In other words, they were allowed to share in their own tithe, but they were reminded not to neglect the Levites who had no inheritance. Not all tithes were brought to the temple; some were designated for certain Levitical cities and taken to places where the people lived. At the end of every third year (the year of tithing), the full tithe of their produce (food) would be brought to be stored within the gates or dwelling places of the Levites. Tithes would help feed strangers, the motherless, the fatherless, and widows.

> "And he commanded the people who lived in Jerusalem to give the portion due to the priests and the Levites, that they might give themselves to the Law of the LORD. As soon as the command was spread abroad, the people of Israel gave in abundance the firstfruits of grain, wine, oil, honey, and of all the produce of the field. And they brought in abundantly the tithe of everything" (2 Chronicles 31:4-5).

The quick takeaway is that the Israelites brought various tithes of food for the purpose of feeding the priestly tribe of the Levites, but also shared in eating it. The *full* tithe requirement was in the third year. And last but not least, it was established as a requirement under the Mosaic law in the Old Covenant.

Considering its true definition, tithing should not be considered a new covenant concept. For one thing, there is no longer a priestly tribe for which to bring a tenth of our food. Although Scripture never makes this declaration, you may have been told the church is the storehouse for tithes under the New Covenant, but this raises many questions. Just exactly how is the church defined, and what is it they are specifically supposed to be given? When did the tithe become about money? Is the church meant to include all individual believers in Christ? Is it a building with a catchy name that has filed for nonprofit status? We tend to forget that God doesn't dwell in church buildings made by human hands (see Acts 17:24-25).

If the tithe should go to those doing the work of the ministry, would this include the many effective laborers who function outside of a corporate church setting? Would the giver of the tithes to the church be allowed to share in eating or spending it as they did under the law? Also make sure the receiver of the tithes doesn't own any property or have another source of income, because that would be a violation of the tithing rules.

The storehouse for Israel under the Old Covenant was just that—a place to store food. In spite of what we've been told, there is no specific storehouse under our current covenant, and it certainly isn't the bank that your church organization does business with at the First Religious Savings & Mistrust. I know Jesus saves, but that's not quite what God had in mind. I'm not even sure whether financial institutions take food deposits, and I seldom see a silo next to a church building.

It is absurd to imply that modern-day ministers under the New Covenant have taken the place of the Jewish priesthood as the designated receivers of tithes. Beware of those who will threaten you with robbing God while they rob you of the truth, by supposing that godliness is a means for financial gain (see 1 Timothy 6:5-10).

The Windows of Heaven

There are those in the legalistic landscape of modern-day religion that have taught the third chapter of Malachi to be understood in a manner something like the following: "If you give ten percent of all your income, you will be blessed. If you neglect this requirement, you will be cursed." You may also have been told that if you give that ten percent, God will open the windows of heaven and bless you with so much financially that you will not be able to contain it. Some teachings will combine spiritual blessings to be included, or take the place of financial blessings. I haven't met a "modern-day tither" yet who had more spiritual blessings and financial return than he or she could contain. That's because Malachi states that the tithe was to be brought so that there would be *food* in the house. As for the *windows of heaven* being opened up, you'll find passages in the Old Testament where that is a reference to rain (see Genesis 7:11, 8:2, 2 Chronicles 7:13 and 1 Kings 8:35).

In other words, God was going to bless their crops and fields by opening the windows of heaven with *rain*, which would result in an abundance of food that would overflow the storehouse. This is why the next verses in

Malachi refer to fruits, vine, soil, and land:

> "I will rebuke the devourer for you, so that it will not destroy the fruits of your soil, and your vine in the field shall not fail to bear, says the LORD of hosts. Then all nations will call you blessed, for you will be a land of delight, says the LORD of hosts" (Malachi 3:11–12).

The Arguments for Tithing Today

There are typically two main arguments frequently heard in favor of tithing. Argument number one: "Jesus said we should tithe." Aside from mentioning the tithe in a parable referring to a self-righteous Pharisee, the only instance of Jesus making a statement about tithing was recorded by both Matthew and Luke. Observe to whom Jesus was speaking, namely *the scribes and Pharisees*. He addresses them by their title at least ten times in Matthew 23, and he had been ripping apart their hypocrisy regarding the Mosaic law throughout the entire chapter: "Woe to you, scribes and Pharisees, hypocrites! For you tithe mint and dill and cumin, and have neglected the weightier matters of the law: justice and mercy and faithfulness. These you ought to have done, without neglecting the others" (Matthew 23:23).

If this is where legalists want to plant their tithing flag, we should all start preparing to bring mint, dill, and cumin to church as part of our tithe. The point is, even Jesus referenced food in relation to the tithe. The Pharisees would meticulously tithe down to the flake or seed of a spice while neglecting heavier matters of the law. Don't skim past what Jesus said about the weightier matters of the law, which included justice, mercy and faithfulness. As good and right as those things are, they were a burden under the law of the first covenant. That's what weightier means— burdensome and heavy (Strong's G926). Yet recall what the Apostle John wrote in his first letter when he stated God's commandments are not *burdensome* (see 1 John 5:3). It's the same Greek word as weightier. Since two different covenants are in play with these passages, *Jesus and John are not talking about the same commandments.*

Clashers will argue Jesus said the Pharisees should still tithe as well, but again, this is at a time when the law was still in effect. Jesus just stated the tithe was part of the law—we aren't under the law! If you think Jesus was instructing us to tithe under the New Covenant, you would also be obligated to abide all the other "law talk" he had been speaking to the Pharisees in the same passage, referring to the altar and the sacrificial offerings on the altar.

Argument number two in favor of tithing: "Abraham (or Abram) tithed before the law." There is one recorded incident of Abraham tithing, and there is no evidence of this being something he practiced on a regular basis. In Genesis 14, we see that he did not tithe from his own possessions but from the spoils of war he had captured. It was done out of his abundance from this, and he did it out of thanksgiving, not by command. He voluntarily gave a tenth to Melchizedek, the priest of God, and voluntarily gave the rest to the king of Sodom.

The seventh chapter of Hebrews is the only place in the epistles of new covenant writings where tithing is mentioned, and it is addressed in the context of Abraham's tithe to Melchizedek. This says nothing about us being required or even encouraged to tithe as a principle to give under the New Covenant. The writer of Hebrews is attempting to show that the Levitical priesthood was not the source that would bring perfection. The mysterious Melchizedek was a type of a higher priesthood likened to the priesthood of Christ. The message isn't about tithing, but is entirely based upon how Christ would be superior to everything, and the entire book of Hebrews is centered on this truth.

Animal sacrifices prior to the law are plentiful, but pre-law tithing was a rarely recorded occurrence such as with Abraham and Jacob, and those were voluntarily of their own free will. Using Abraham as a trophy for tithing is the equivalent to saying we should still sacrifice animals, because he did that, too. As animal sacrifices became a part of the law, so did the tithe. Start counting the number of Scriptures in the New Covenant teaching us to tithe and sacrifice animals. Trust me, you won't need a calculator.

Regardless of what curses came through the former covenant, redemption has occurred from all of them through Christ. With this in mind, it's time to consider one of the most exciting ideals of living under a new and better covenant—the ministry of giving.

(14) GRACE GIVING

SOMETIMES IN GRACE, people only see what they are released from without realizing what they have been brought *into*. In other words, it's possible to begin recognizing the blessings of what is no longer required, while missing the purpose of what it means to be a new creation. It's not just about being free from what you don't have to do, but it's also coming to an awareness of a new motivation you'll have in Christ, or discovering a *desire* to allow the Lord to express himself in and through you.

Considering what has just been addressed about tithing, let's touch briefly on the blessing and opportunity we have to participate in *giving gracefully* under this New Covenant. I have a great appreciation for those who have devoted their lives to ministry. What I have stated about the tithe and the Christian religious system in general is not meant to be a personal attack on them or the church of Jesus Christ. Much of what gets taught today is the result of ministers passing on what they learned from others before them, whether right or wrong.

It is not my goal to discourage people from giving, but to encourage it even more from a perspective of grace and love. As a new creation in Christ, part of the nature and identity we possess is to be free to love and free to give, usually in that order. God loved the world so much that he gave his only begotten Son. True love inspires selfless, joyous, heartfelt giving. This is why it's so important for us to grasp and experience what God has given to us with his love, life, liberty and mercy. It is difficult to give to others what you don't have or what you are not aware of possessing.

Getting some context from Paul, he addresses believers in Corinth about supplying needs for others. There was a planned ministry of giving taking place, and he is writing to these folks who previously had indicated their intent to give generously to others in need. He was sending people ahead to confirm they were prepared to minister their giving as previously promised. Right after Paul's exhortation about this, he continues: "The point is this: whoever sows sparingly will also reap sparingly, and whoever sows bountifully will also reap bountifully" (2 Corinthians 9:6).

Often we're told this means if we sow much money or material things, we will reap an abundance of money and material things in return. By the same token, we're told if we sow sparingly with our giving, our rate of return (or reaping) will bring much less to us. But take a step back and consider what it is that's being sown, and just as importantly, what it is that's being reaped or harvested. Once we get the focus off of ourselves and consider the well-being of others, the answer is not exactly rocket science—sow bountifully and you will reap a bountiful blessing for those who are being *sown into*. Likewise, if you sow sparingly, you will reap a smaller blessing for those who are on the receiving end. I'm aware this is not how the passage is usually regarded, so the rest of this chapter will attempt to provide a view of the bigger picture for you to examine on the subject of giving.

There are those appearing as shepherds who will pray outwardly, when inwardly they are wolves seeking their prey. Some of them are in charge of the local sheep farm (church), or as they might like to call it, the storehouse. If you've been told that you'll reap more money because you plant (give) more money, this is a misleading twist of the Scriptures that wanders from the truth and usually comes from people with their hand out.

Jesus said to give to the needy in secret, suggesting that the approach to giving should not be concentrated as much on the giver, but on those in need. Certainly God supplies seed to the sower, but his blessings arrive to us freely by his grace, not by us doing something that causes us to think we deserve it—otherwise it isn't grace, but becomes something earned through a work. Fortunately, that's not how it works in the New Covenant.

The Law of Sowing and Reaping

There is a natural law of sowing and reaping, but try not to adopt the mindset that it is entirely identical with the gospel. Many religions will use this "law" to hammer a message that says "If you do good, then good things will happen to you. Do bad things and bad things will happen to you." *This isn't the gospel.* In this fallen world, often we see where terrible things happen to loving, decent people, and vice versa.

While the assumption is made that we will personally reap whatever we sow, good and bad are often open to interpretation, depending on the brand of religion. I'm not a gambler, but I can parade a significant string of witnesses that will testify they sowed into a slot machine without reaping anything in return. However, *someone else* did reap from what they sowed. I know some will not like my gambling illustration, but it has parallels to misleading prosperity teaching that has turned God into a vending machine, as if you can put something in and he will automatically give you something back. Those who have been victims of such manipulative methods have found themselves experiencing what I call the law of "rowing and seeping." People have been told they are cursed and lack blessings for not tithing or they are not giving enough, so they work diligently to give and then give some more in order to try to make it work, but they can never seem to get the boat to float. When they don't reap, they might be told it is because they did not give with enough faith. This keeps the carrot dangling in front of them, although it will seem to remain just out of their reach.

Grace has allowed us to reap good things we did not deserve, where we did not sow or labor. Likewise, mercy has granted us *not* to reap or experience punishment from what we have sown or deserved. The good news for us is that Jesus reaped what we sowed (our corruption) and he died. In return, we reaped what he has sown (his life), and now we live. Jesus said this to his followers:

> "Already he who reaps is receiving wages and is gathering fruit for life eternal; so that he who sows and he who reaps may rejoice together. Thus the saying 'One sows and another reaps' is true. I sent you to reap what you have not worked for. Others have done the hard work, and you have reaped the benefits of their labor"

(John 4:36–38 NASB).

Although the phrase never appears in Scripture, you'll find plenty of things written and taught by others about "the law of sowing and reaping." The subject gets twisted by well-meaning people trying to paste a lot of different Bible verses together, and we'd have to address most of it in a book of its own. If we really reaped *everything* we sowed, it would bring us to a place of condemnation and then damnation. It would plant us back under a ministry of works where we'd spin our wheels in hopes that our good would outweigh our bad, and the fruit of our own labor would tip the scales far enough for God to accept us or bless us. It's the old mentality of thinking God is grading us on a curve, comparing us to others. There is sowing by some and there is reaping by others, but let's leave "the law" out of it.

Here is a passage that gets quoted frequently on the subject of the law of sowing and reaping:

> "Do not be deceived: God is not mocked, for whatever one sows, that will he also reap. For the one who sows to his own flesh will from the flesh reap corruption, but the one who sows to the Spirit will from the Spirit reap eternal life. And let us not grow weary of doing good, for in due season we will reap, if we do not give up" (Galatians 6:7–9).

Stepping back from the trees to get some context within the previous chapter, we discover a contrast of the flesh and the Spirit, "But if you are led by the Spirit, you are not under the Law" (Galatians 5:18). The fruit of the Spirit also occurs apart from the law. We're exhorted to avoid being boastful which leads to envy and challenging one another. Instead we should minister restoration to each other and bear one another's burdens. We shouldn't grow weary in doing good to all people, and by sowing these things we "fulfill the law of Christ" (Galatians 6:2). That's the law we're under—the law of the Spirit of Life found in Christ Jesus where faith works through love, not the law of sowing and reaping. Let's pause to ask ourselves a question: *Why would Paul contradict himself by telling the Galatians they were free from the law of works, and then in the next breath submit they are under a law of sowing and reaping based upon what they do?*

I'm not suggesting our actions and choices are insignificant or unimportant, but don't get caught placing yourself under so-called laws that have roots going back to the same law the Jewish people were freed from. Don't confuse the consequences of poor decision making in this world with how God relates to you in Christ. Anything that implies, "I will receive good or bad from God because of what I do" is a step back to the previous covenant. It implies we'll get what we deserve, which is actually the opposite of God's grace. It was for freedom that Christ set us free. When we sow to the Spirit, we simply trust in what he does instead of ourselves, and what is it we reap? Eternal life! This has nothing to do with our good works.

The primary emphasis from the fifth and sixth chapters of Galatians is comparing the works of the flesh with the fruit of Spirit. Sowing to the Spirit brings grace, mercy and eternal life apart from the law of works. Sowing to the flesh can involve sinful activity, but at other times it may actually appear as good and spiritual outwardly (think of the Pharisees). You can sow to the flesh with your efforts and have good intentions, but it is a double-edged sword because the reaping will provide you with what is truly deserved, and profits nothing in the end. In the kingdom, we know that anything we reap is due to the work of Christ. In grace, we no longer sow to benefit only ourselves but to be a blessing to others. As Paul reminds us in Philippians 2:3, "Do nothing from selfish ambition or conceit, but in humility count others more significant than yourselves."

Good Measure, Pressed Down

Another passage often taken out of context when applied to the subject of giving is when Jesus said this in Luke 6:38: "Give, and it will be given to you. Good measure, pressed down, shaken together, running over, will be put into your lap. For with the measure you use it will be measured back to you."

That's another one of those island verses I often hear quoted, and it is especially applied as a standard for new covenant giving while frequently using money as the motivation to get more back. I'm not anti-prosperity, nor am I down on God blessing people. In fact, I believe he wants to provide an abundance of good things into our lives because he is the ultimate giver. But this method used by motivational prosperity speakers or ministers to manipulate others into giving is missing the point of the passage. It is just another example of the power of being able to sell people almost anything if you can make it sound like it's true.

In looking at the eight verses prior to Luke 6:38, it appears similar to a rerun of the Sermon on the Mount, where Jesus was in the middle of hammering the law as we saw in Matthew. In those verses, Jesus said to treat others the same way you wanted them to treat you, give to everyone who asks, and if someone takes what belongs to you, don't demand it back. He went on to say that if you love those who love you, even sinners can behave in that way. If you lend, expecting something back, what credit is that to you? Even sinners can lend while expecting to receive back the same amount. In addition to communicating all of this, Jesus continues:

> "But love your enemies, and do good, and lend, expecting nothing in return, and your reward will be great, and you will be sons of the Most High, for he is kind to the ungrateful and the evil. Judge not, and you will not be judged; condemn not, and you will not be condemned; forgive, and you will be forgiven" (Luke 6:35–37).

Once again in context, we see some real solid law teaching here from Jesus, including forgiveness based only upon certain conditions. Luke 6:38 is usually used as a basis to motivate people to give more, especially money. They are taught the more you give, the more you'll get back. That thought process is the opposite of what Jesus said leading up to this because he just got done saying to do good, and even when lending to your enemies, expect nothing in return. True giving is selfless and doesn't seek a reward. It's time to take a breath and ask ourselves a question: *How can we lend or give, not expecting anything in return, and then suddenly start giving with the purpose and motivation of getting something back?*

If you're giving anything for the *purpose* of receiving for yourself, then you've fallen back under law. Religion has it backwards. We don't give with the motivation of receiving blessings for ourselves; we freely receive blessings from God that we have not earned or deserved, and *then* we freely give. Similarly, as revealed earlier, we don't forgive in order to receive forgiveness, but receive forgiveness (from God) and then are able to forgive others in return. As we yield and trust in the Spirit of God within, he orchestrates his will through us. This is why Paul said, "So neither he who plants nor he who waters is anything, but only God who gives the growth" (1 Corinthians 3:7). Some will lay a foundation and others will build upon it, but it's the same Lord of love working through both.

How Much Should You Give?

Here is the question we should be asking: What is the standard for giving under the New Covenant? The answer? Whatever your heart desires! In 2 Corinthians 9:7, Paul says, "Each one must give as he has decided in his heart, not reluctantly or under compulsion, for God loves a cheerful giver."

In spite of all the tithing talk and different viewpoints on the subject, Paul specifically just laid out the best definition of giving under the New Covenant. Each person decides freely within their own heart how much they want to give. Covenant clashers will sound the alarm that it won't be enough unless people are commanded to give a certain percentage. Freedom is a powerful thing, and it will actually cause us to place our trust in the One who supplies us with the resources to give.

I fully understand the concern from ministers for feeling the need to provide people with a reason to give in order for the ministry to function. My exhortation to pastors and teachers is to help people realize who they are as a new creation in Christ. Instead of threatening them with a curse, they can be encouraged on why to give freely from a perspective of love and compassion, as it has been placed on their hearts to do so. Instead of seeing people through the lens of a former covenant that demanded individual obedience to the point of perfection, begin to view those you serve as righteous, perfected, and one with Christ. When they hear it taught, they will begin to believe it, and when they do, it can change everything in their lives for the better.

We should give because grace has supplied us with the desire to do it.

Paul continues to exhort the believers of the church in Corinth to let grace rule in their giving. Not only does our generosity supply those in need, but it results in thanksgiving to God by those who are beneficiaries of the gifts.

> "And God is able to make all grace abound to you, so that having all sufficiency in all things at all times, you may abound in every good work. He who supplies seed to the sower and bread for food will supply and multiply your seed for sowing and increase the harvest of your righteousness. You will be enriched in every way to be generous in every way, which through us will produce thanksgiving to God. For the ministry of this service is not only supplying the needs of the saints but is also overflowing in many thanksgivings to God" (2 Corinthians 9:8, 10-12).

I hope we understand that giving and contributions are necessary in this world in order for ministry to move forward to others. This especially applies to helping those who are in need and lacking. God is the one who can make all grace abound, exceedingly in abundance, so that we can sufficiently have all the necessities in life and have our seed multiplied in order to help supply for others in need.

I'm not at all suggesting it's wrong to have money or resources stored up, but the harvest that is reaped isn't for the purpose of our own bank account. It is the manifestation of this grace *for others* to experience, and their giving of thanks *to God* because of your generosity. Paul mentioned this earlier in the same letter: "For it is all for your sake, so that as grace extends to more and more people it may increase thanksgiving, to the glory of God" (2 Corinthians 4:15).

Giving is not about trying to be noticed. It's not so you can toot your trumpet in front of the church congregation and brag about God blessing you with more simply because you gave more. That approach puts law-like conditions on our giving and will lead to boasting, instead of faith working through love. It will also lead to envy, while provoking and irritating one another.

A harvest is reaped so grace and the righteousness of God can spread. Why not let yourself be the vessel through which God ministers to others!

We should be humbled and consider it an honor to be used in this way. The Lord of the harvest (or the Lord of the reaping) is looking to increase his storehouse with *people* (see Matthew 9:37–38). The people themselves *are* the harvest for the storehouse in the kingdom of God.

I don't want to discourage anyone from giving ten percent of their income, but this is not defined as a tithe. It's simply an amount you have decided you feel comfortable with and are joyful to give. If you have decided within your heart to give a certain percentage of your intake, that is your choice, as is to whom and where you give. You may decide to give more or less, but it is built into you to be generous with what you have been given.

Peter once looked at a man who was lame and was begging for money. "But Peter said, 'I have no silver and gold, but what I do have I give to you. In the name of Jesus Christ of Nazareth, rise up and walk!' " (Acts 3:6).

Peter met his physical needs with something that was better than money in this instance, and we can do the same. We can share love, mercy, kindness, forgiveness, talent, food, goods, time, and more. Even if you have been limited financially, you have other gifts or talents to sow and contribute. Do it because you *want to* and feel good about it! You are now free in Him, and there are no limits to what God can do through you.

(15) CHANGING YOUR THINKING (REPENTANCE)

R EPENTANCE IS SOMETHING ELSE we hear much about in Christian circles, and often we grace renegades are accused of not encouraging it enough. As dedicated people of grace, we most certainly believe in repentance; after all, repentance from dead works is an elementary teaching when it comes to the gospel of Christ. But just exactly what is repentance? In the world where covenants collide, repentance has evolved to mean we need to do something about our sin. However, let's define the true meaning of repentance and how it applies to our lives in the New Covenant.

> "Now after John was arrested, Jesus came into Galilee, proclaiming the gospel of God, and saying, 'The time is fulfilled, and the kingdom of God is at hand; repent and believe in the gospel' " (Mark 1:14–15).

Look again at the above passage in Mark. If the basic meaning of *repent* means to turn from your sin, then Jesus had it backwards, because he said repent first and then believe. If we're supposed to start out repenting by stopping the bad stuff and getting cleaned up, this suggests we need to make ourselves presentable and acceptable to God *before* we believe, which implies salvation is not a gift. But even the legalistic mindset within most corners of Christianity will usually agree we come to belief in Christ *first*.

This is one of those contradictions I butted heads with prior to realizing the grace of the gospel. When Jesus said "repent," he didn't have it backwards, but the religious world has tried to turn this inside out. The way to repent is by believing in something different—in this case, the gospel.

Much of the confusion about repentance is connected to the English definition of the word that defines it as "to have sorrow and deep regret for sin." We've all experienced that sort of thing to some degree, but this is not how the word *repent* is defined in the original language. I'm not a Greek language scholar, but others much smarter than I will agree that the true biblical definition for *repent* is not the same as we find in our English dictionary. For example, we're often told repentance means "to stop sinning and start living differently." This is the equivalent of treating the symptom and not the cause.

The word *repent* is from the Greek word *metanoeo*, and it is merely defined as *to have a change of mind* (Strong's G3340). It originates from another word that simply means *to think, consider* (Strong's G3539). Hitherto and henceforth, the word *repent* literally means to think, accompanied by a change of mind, leading one to perceive things differently. It is often assumed a change of mind leads to a change of action. While that's not the purest definition of repentance, the change of mind that occurs will result in you putting a halt to trying to improve your position with God (based on your own merit) and begin trusting in what God did through Christ on your behalf.

You see, repentance is not so much about trying to turn from wicked works to improve yourself. Instead, repentance is the withdrawal from trying to earn favor with God through dead works, while trusting in *his* work by faith. This change of mind can allow for a shift into a completely different gear, while becoming a game changer in your life.

Covenant clashers will erroneously assume we're saying it's okay to sin, or that it doesn't matter whether we turn from sin or not. This is not what we're saying. However, repentance that leads to salvation doesn't specifically mean to turn from your sins, and it doesn't mean a change in behavior. Yet some modern Bible translations such as the New Living Translation have changed the phrasing to imply this, but it's based on the assumption that the word, *repent,* means to turn from sins. It's simply not accurate in the original language. Here is an example of this from a verse found in the NLT (Matthew 3:2): "Turn from your sins and turn to God, because the Kingdom of Heaven is near."

Compare that to other common and respected translations, such as NASB, KJV, NKJV, NIV, ESV, and RSV, all of which have a matching or very similar translation such as this: "Repent, for the kingdom of heaven is at hand."

See the difference? They were told that it was time to change their mind and believe the good news. Change their thinking from what? Naturally, it would be to turn from doing what they'd been attempting to do for centuries by trying to attain right standing with God through the works of the law. When Jesus showed up to start his ministry, remember the message was first meant for Israel, whom Jesus came to redeem from the curse of the law they were under. He wasn't speaking to Gentiles or Samaritans, or even "good Samaritans" (see Matthew 10-5-6). Surely his purpose wasn't just to tell these people they needed to try harder with this law thing and start doing it better, because "better" isn't what God was after. He was looking for *perfection*, and it was found in Jesus Christ, who is the end of the law for righteousness to all who believe.

Avoiding sin is always good advice, but repentance goes much deeper than that. For centuries, the Jewish people were consumed daily with trying to do it right through hundreds of burdensome commandments in which they couldn't begin to measure up to the required standard. There was no lack of sin consciousness with this bunch, but they kept trying anyway. After all, they were bound to a covenant they took very seriously, even though they consistently failed. So when we talk about repenting, Jesus wasn't just specifically referring to people being sorry for their sins (verb), but rather turning from a consciousness of sin (noun) that was rooted in their failure to abide by all things written in the law. Under the replacement covenant, we begin to realize now that in him, we are dead to sin. This would occur without all the sacrifices and sin confessions.

Sin Management

With every head bowed and every eye closed, let me see a show of hands: Have you behaved and performed *perfectly* within the past week or month without committing some type of sinful action or wrong thought? Based on *religion's* definition of repentance—meaning to turn from sin—you haven't repented. Perhaps you've reduced your sin count, but if this is your understanding of repentance, you've fallen into the trap of thinking your good works need to outweigh your bad in order to attain or maintain any combination of justification, sanctification, forgiveness, fellowship, and so on. This is not repentance.

Regardless of one's religious affiliation, a person can attempt to turn from sin without ever believing in Jesus Christ. They can "repent" by aiming to improve their behavior, do it better than almost anyone else, and still remain an unbeliever. Some of the nicest and most moral people I know are not even professing Christians. Religion's definition of repentance has trained us on trying to fix what is broken and making up for our mistakes. While this seems like it's the correct mindset, it only leads to the flesh, whereas true repentance will always be a response to the grace of what *God* has done through Jesus Christ on our behalf. You are not the fixer.

To avoid any confusion, *repentance* can have different meanings in the Old Testament and translates a bit differently from what we have in the language of the New Testament. It may come as a surprise that the word *repent* or *repented* only appears approximately 15 times in the entire Old Testament of the NASB. The Hebrew word appearing most often means "to turn back or to return" (Strong's H7725). This word appears more than a thousand times in the Old Testament, but only about one percent of the time is it translated as the word *repent*. The rest of the time it was translated into dozens and dozens of different words and phrases with a variety of meanings, including a change of mind, but mainly projects the idea of turning. On several occasions, another Hebrew word is used and it is defined as "to be sorry, console oneself" (Strong's H5162).

In the first covenant, that's what people had to work with—sorrow and consoling themselves, along with the blood of bulls and goats which couldn't take away sin. The rich young ruler was sorrowful because he had tried to earn eternal life through the works of the law. If he had sold everything and given it away, this would not have been a form of repentance but just another attempt at keeping the law. In order to reach his desired destination, he would need to repent by having a change of mind and turning from that endeavor. *Jesus has borne our griefs and carried our sorrows* (see Isaiah 53:4).

If My People

I hesitate to mention yet another Bible verse that is often considered to be sacred ground, but in order to help us recognize there are two covenants that are not alike, let's take a fresh look at what God said to Solomon after the holy temple was built:

> "When I shut up the heavens so that there is no rain, or command the locust to devour the land, or send pestilence among my people, (14) if my people who are called by my name humble themselves, and pray and seek my face and turn from their wicked ways, then I will hear from heaven and will forgive their sin and heal their land" (2 Chronicles 7:13–14).

Quite often we find where verse 14 is quoted as a directive for people from the current generation of *today*. We're told to pray, seek God, and turn from sinning so that we will be forgiven, and our land will be healed. In other words, according to covenant clashers, forgiveness and blessings for us would be based upon certain conditions. Religion has taught that the target audience here is pointing to believers belonging to any nation, but look through the entire chapter (and the previous chapter) and begin to see where this was clearly addressing "my people" who were in a covenant with God at that time—referring to the nation of Israel. Some might say, "If it was good enough for Israel, it's good enough for us." That would be fine and dandy ... if there had been only one covenant.

> "Now my eyes will be open and my ears attentive to the prayer that is made in this place. For now I have chosen and consecrated this house that my name may be there forever. My eyes and my heart will be there for all time" (2 Chronicles 7:15–16).

The passage in this chapter centers around prayer being heard from the temple that was just constructed. God said his ears would hear the prayer being made in that place and he declared it would be a house of sacrifice. During the grand opening, Solomon dedicated the temple with a sacrificial offering of 22,000 oxen and 120,000 sheep, but the neighbors weren't complaining. Perhaps the "fire works" that came down from heaven had something to do with that. This was a celebration which had expectations at a new high—at least for a little while.

God proceeded to tell Solomon to do according to all that he commanded, including the keeping of his statutes and rules. Turning aside from *any* of the commandments would result in the need to be seeking the face of God and his forgiveness all over again. That's just how it was in the Old Covenant.

"Religious" repentance is often linked by clashers to 2 Chronicles 7:14, and I agree that we should repent. The way to do this is by changing our thinking because under a better covenant established upon better promises, forgiveness and blessings for us did *not* arrive by seeking God's face through prayer or improving our behavior to a higher standard through works of the law; nor did it come by sacrificing animals, but rather through Jesus Christ and his shed blood. Under the first covenant, the Jews would seek forgiveness that was *temporary*, but now we no longer need to seek the face of God at the temple in the hopes that he will hear us from heaven. With the final sacrifice of Christ, the temple veil was torn in two from top to bottom and he abides in us by the life of his Spirit.

There are some mindsets we've established for ourselves where it is hard to let go, and this one from the second book of Chronicles will be tough for many who are stuck in covenant confusion. But that's okay! For anyone sincerely interested in wanting to have a greater knowledge of the truth (Jesus), this will force one to begin asking questions that religious tradition has a hard time answering. For example, why would God continue to repeatedly forgive the sin of the people in a new covenant where he remembers sin no more? Allow the Spirit to be your teacher. As we grow in the grace of God, hopefully we can begin to comprehend the gospel is not about us—it's all about him.

Since we no longer need to seek an "elusive" God, nor do we have to petition him for his love, acceptance and forgiveness, a better approach to prayer under the New Covenant would be something like this:

> "First of all, then, I urge that supplications, prayers, intercessions, and thanksgivings be made for all people, for kings and all who are in high positions, that we may lead a peaceful and quiet life, godly and dignified in every way" (1 Timothy 2:1-2).

God has provided us with heavenly peace—he is our peace! But we're living in a fallen world, and it would be good for us to take the advice of the Apostle Paul and pray for those who are in positions of authority; who desire to govern and rule over our lives, so we can live a peaceful life here on earth.

Repentance and Forgiveness

After the resurrection, Jesus appeared to his disciples to show them his body and that he had risen.

> "Then he said to them, 'These are my words that I spoke to you while I was still with you, that everything written about me in the Law of Moses and the Prophets and the Psalms must be fulfilled.' Then he opened their minds to understand the Scriptures, and said to them, 'Thus it is written, that the Christ should suffer and on the third day rise from the dead, and that repentance and forgiveness of sins should be proclaimed in his name to all nations, beginning from Jerusalem. You are witnesses of these things. And behold, I am sending the promise of my Father upon you. But stay in the city until you are clothed with power from on high' " (Luke 24:44-49).

It's intriguing how Jesus stated the Old Testament writings foretold of his rising from the dead on the third day. Can you find such a specific passage? Probably not, but it's in there. Jesus referred to the story of Jonah as one example, but we usually aren't connecting Jesus to those old writings because we assume they are just interesting stories or thoughts about something else (also see Genesis 22:4; Hosea 6:2; 1 Corinthians 15:4).

Jesus took his boys through the law of Moses, the Prophets, and the Psalms, and he connected all the dots so they could see the big picture. What a picture that must have been! He reminded them how all of those things had to be fulfilled. You may recall that this is what he started off with near the beginning of The Sermon on the Mount, and now after the resurrection, they *were* fulfilled.

Notice how Jesus said repentance *and* the forgiveness of sins should be proclaimed, not repentance *to get* forgiveness. A change of law would bring a change of priesthood, which would bring a change in forgiveness (once and for all), which would result in the need to have a change of mind. Although some translations state repentance *for* the forgiveness of sins, this should be interpreted *because of* the forgiveness of sins. This can apply to other passages when it comes to repentance, such as when Peter proclaimed Christ right after the Holy Spirit came upon them:

> "And Peter said to them, 'Repent and be baptized every one of you in the name of Jesus Christ for the forgiveness of your sins, and you will receive the gift of the Holy Spirit. For the promise is for you and for your children and for all who are far off, everyone whom the Lord our God calls to himself' " (Acts 2:38–39).

Peter is telling the people of Jerusalem to change their mind and be baptized in the name of Jesus Christ *because of* the forgiveness of sins—not in order *to get* forgiveness. If the latter were true, we would have all kinds of contradictions in the Scripture, and we know that is not the case. You may have noticed, Peter stated that this forgiveness and gift of the Spirit included those Gentiles who had been *far off.*

On a side note ... when we see the word baptism, it doesn't always mean being dipped into water. Baptism in water is simply an outward demonstration of something that has inwardly already occurred. It symbolizes how we were baptized or placed into the body of Christ, died with him and have been raised with him. It's a response to the forgiveness that has been bought and paid for with the blood of Christ. By the way, for your own future study, you may find it interesting that the Israelites were baptized into Moses (see 1 Corinthians 10:2). You weren't meant to be baptized into Christ and then sprinkled with old covenant commandments that came through Moses. Meditate on this and it may cause a light to shine in the corners of your mind where it had not previously seen the connection.

People will often ask what good the Old Testament is for us who are under the New Covenant. Remember the three things Jesus used in teaching his students. If it helps, imagine Dorothy and her friends from *The Wizard of Oz* walking down the yellow brick road of Emmaus chanting repeatedly, "Moses, the Prophets, and Psalms, oh my!" Quite often I will hear verses quoted from those old passages as people attempt to apply them to their personal lives. Although it may be relevant to do so in some cases, I believe they are often connected more to Jesus Christ than to us, including the Psalms. Keep it in mind the next time you're visiting that area of the forest.

Shortly after Philip joined as a disciple, he quickly discovered a connection between Jesus and who the Scriptures spoke of in regards to the Messiah. "Philip found Nathanael and said to him, 'We have found him of whom Moses in the Law and also the prophets wrote, Jesus of Nazareth, the son of Joseph' " (John 1:45). This is why we don't toss aside those old covenant passages; they were not given for the purpose of simply gaining comfort or to see the history of the events with some really interesting stories. *It was the mystery of Christ contained in those Scriptures which would later be revealed.* It can be hard to understand it all, and although much of the Old Testament is not meant directly for believers in Christ from a covenant perspective, there is a fascinating road map showing how we arrived at this place of grace. But it's not meant to be a compass for Christians on how to get to the destination. We've already arrived at our destination—Jesus Christ.

Jesus told the disciples to go and teach what he taught them, but we don't have a record of everything Jesus taught in Matthew, Mark, Luke, and John. A case in point is how he just took them through the Law, the Prophets, and the Psalms, but we don't have all the specifics of what he revealed to his pupils. To get an idea of what Jesus taught them, look at the writings *after* those four books. Start on *this* side of the cross and then find your way back to compare it to what Jesus said as a man on the earth. This may help determine the context of what Jesus was saying while taking into consideration whom he was talking to. Was it the old law, or was he pointing to something new that was to come? Does it seem to contradict the writings of the New Covenant? Don't get so caught up staring at the individual verses of the four gospels without referring to the revelation of the new covenant Scriptures that appear after those books. It will change your thinking.

The good news of the gospel may seem as though it's too good to be true. But repentance isn't about your performance or following religious rules. Genuine repentance is to have a change of mind and believe that Jesus did it all on our behalf.

(16) LIFE IN THE NEW COVENANT

I N MY EARLY TEEN YEARS when my voice began to change, it did so quickly and substantially. A couple of squeaks ... and suddenly I sounded like that deep voice coming from the burning bush in the movie whose title seems to have escaped me for the moment. In speaking to my Mom, my voice sounded so different that she thought I was trying to fake it with my new pipes, and she cut me off in the middle of a sentence with a scolding voice, "Stop talking like that!" It wasn't much different after I came to an increased maturity through a revelation of the gospel of grace and my newfound identity. I had a couple of squeaks and then began sounding different in what I was communicating about it. The results were the same—in that church folks everywhere began telling me to "stop talking like that."

Grace Warning!

Curiously, we have leaders within Christian ministry who teach a religious doctrine that *promotes* the very thing that brings death, condemnation, and bondage, and causes sin to increase. Think about that for a minute. They are endorsing and recommending a failed system that has proven to result in more sinning! In addition to this, and equally as startling, is something that should raise all kinds of red flags—these same Bible teachers will warn you about the "dangers" of what they consider to be excessive grace. It doesn't take a biblical scholar to recognize there is

CLASH OF THE COVENANTS

something wrong with this picture. The notion that grace without law will cause people to fall into sin and lead them into lasciviousness is a lie from the enemy, a figment of the imagination exalting itself against the knowledge of God, and it needs to be cast down. The origin of such talk comes from a source of deep darkness. Suggesting you can have too much emphasis on grace is to say you can have too much of Jesus—and that is where the real danger lies.

We've discovered what it is that actually arouses sinful passions and causes sin to increase, and I can assure you it is *not* grace. In fact, here is what grace will do:

> "For the grace of God has appeared, bringing salvation for all people, training us to renounce ungodliness and worldly passions, and to live self-controlled, upright, and godly lives in the present age" (Titus 2:11-12).

Grace was manifested in the person of Jesus Christ, so when grace appeared, it was Christ who appeared. The essence of grace *is contained* in Jesus Christ. Words can have different meanings, but when defined biblically under the New Covenant, you can't have grace without Jesus, because he *is* grace. The Hebrew language of the Old Testament doesn't describe grace in the same way as what we have under the New Covenant. It is difficult to accurately describe something not personally experienced, or someone not personally known.

It's hard to fathom why people who call themselves Christians would ever get the idea that an excess of grace is a problem. Grace is the one thing that leads us to salvation and inspires the desire for godly living. In the land of the legal, religionists will express nervousness and concern with those who they believe are hyper about grace, yet give them something with a little law mixed in for "balance," and everything will be fine with the world. Those dots are not properly connected, and this results in a distorted picture of the gospel.

I have some breaking news that just came in a couple of thousand years ago—*there is no balance between law and grace.* "For sin will have no dominion over you, since you are not under law but under grace" (Romans

6:14). You are either under law or under grace, but you can't have it both ways. You can't tout grace one minute, and then contradict it with the law of sin and death the next minute. The legalists call for a balance between the two does not hold up in Scripture when we understand the difference between the two covenants. You can embrace the cross or Sinai ... choose wisely.

This is not a matter of pitting grace *against* the law, but recognizing grace *apart* from law. Since you died with Christ, the focus isn't meant to be on your ability to perform, but on the foundation built upon the One who lives in you. As Paul puts it in Galatians 2:20:

> "I have been crucified with Christ. It is no longer I who live, but Christ who lives in me. And the life I now live in the flesh I live by faith in the Son of God, who loved me and gave himself for me."

The accusation by Christian religionists who claim we're hyper about grace is meant to be critical and even insulting. The charge implies grace can be taken to an extreme beyond what is needed. With the term *hyper-grace*, their allegations of false doctrine and heresy are hollow, because what they are actually doing is accurately defining the true meaning of God's grace. Reconsider Romans 5:20: "Now the law came in to increase the trespass, but where sin increased, grace abounded all the more." The word *abounded* is from the Greek word *huperperisseuo*, which means to "exceed and overflow" (Strong's G5248). It comes from two words put together; *huper* is where we get the English prefix "hyper," and means beyond and above. The other word, *perisseuo*, means to exceed what is necessary. In other words, whenever you say "grace" before a meal, there should always be leftovers! It's no wonder there were baskets filled with food after going on a picnic with Jesus. Thankfully for us, grace *is* hyper!

Obedience or Grace?

Covenant clashing legalists will toss Bible bones to those who are starving for righteousness and living in the fear of wondering where they stand with God. One example is something like this: "Grace did not save Noah, obedience did." We can avoid injury from these incoming missiles by bringing the gospel into the "mix."

"Noah found grace in the eyes of the Lord" (Genesis 6:8 NKJV). Grace is always the root for every kind of true obedience. With this in mind, the writer of Hebrews spent ten chapters explaining the New Covenant, and then looks back upon Noah's experience:

> "By faith Noah, being warned by God concerning events as yet unseen, in reverent fear constructed an ark for the saving of his household. By this he condemned the world and became an heir of the righteousness that comes by faith" (Hebrews 11:7).

The key words from the passages above are grace, faith and heir of righteousness. These aren't credited to us (or Noah) by our doing. In the covenant where we abide, we have received grace which brings about the obedience of faith (see Romans 1:5). Obedience is a wonderful thing, but it isn't by *our* obedience that anyone is saved, it was from the obedience of Christ that we are made righteous (see Romans 5:19).

Noah responded to grace by faith. Obedience by faith (not works) is what we're talking about here (see Romans 16:25-27). If you try to separate grace and faith from obedience, it will lead to boasting in one's efforts, which came to an end in the new covenant of Christ.

A License to Sin?

Those embedded with a legalistic point of view can't get past their concern that "too much grace talk" will give people a license to sin. Of course, there is no specific sin license that is issued, not by grace or anything else. People will somehow manage to sin rather effortlessly without the need of a license. A "license to sin" is a fabrication born from a legalistic gospel of confusion, and it simply does not exist.

In the land of the legal, they have this entire license thing backwards. A license gives you the right or permission to do something. As we saw in Titus, grace does not advocate doing what is wrong. Grace inspires something more significant than duty or obligation. It inspires love which motivates a sincere desire to contribute for the good, and the giving of ourselves. *The fear that grace gives too much freedom to make wrong choices is a false accusation and a myth.* We are free to make right and wrong choices, but don't blame grace (Jesus) just because someone got carried away by their own lust and fleshly thinking.

Evidently Paul had this accusation thrown at him about giving people a license to sin when it came to the subject of free grace. On several occasions, he addressed this and attempted to explain our position as believers in Christ:

> "What shall we say then? Are we to continue in sin that grace may abound? By no means! How can we who died to sin still live in it? Do you not know that all of us who have been baptized into Christ Jesus were baptized into his death?" (Romans 6:1-3).

We don't attempt to avoid sin by following the commandment that brought death, because we died with Jesus and have been raised to walk in newness of life. We often fail to grasp that we are dead to sin. While covenant clashers will presume to think the message of grace apart from law is an implication that it's okay to sin, they fail to recognize it is the same accusation the enemy will use, because it's one of the few strategies of deception Satan has left against grace.

> "For you were called to freedom, brothers. Only do not use your freedom as an opportunity for the flesh, but through love serve one another. For the whole law is fulfilled in one word: 'You shall love your neighbor as yourself.' But if you bite and devour one another, watch out that you are not consumed by one another" (Galatians 5:13-15).

This is an excellent example of Paul exhorting those of us who are in Christ to do what is right *by living from the identity we have inherited from him.* But don't get caught staring at the tree of verse 14, which quoted a commandment from the Old Covenant, and think now we can assume Paul is the new poster child for the Mosaic law. No, he just spent the past four chapters in Galatians explaining deliverance from the entire law, including the commandments that brought bondage from Mt. Sinai. Here is the point of the context: If they could have kept that one command (love your neighbor as yourself), they would've been able to fulfill the entire law package.

In Christ, we have been born in him with a perfect love, a built-in desire to do what's right because this is who we've been made to be as a new creation. *But we're freely choosing to do it from a relationship of love, not because it's being demanded of us.* If our main purpose in the Christian life is to try to follow marching orders under the command, it probably isn't authentic love.

Contrary to the old way, the covenant of Christ now allows us to depend on a new heart and the new life into which we've been transferred. Paul continues the theme in Galatians, emphasizing that we now walk by the Spirit and are not under the law:

> "But I say, walk by the Spirit, and you will not gratify the desires of the flesh. For the desires of the flesh are against the Spirit, and the desires of the Spirit are against the flesh, for these are opposed to each other, to keep you from doing the things you want to do. But if you are led by the Spirit, you are not under the law" (Galatians 5:16–18).

I often hear statements like this from those caught in the tangled web of legalanity: "But people need those rules to guide them and keep them accountable!" I guess this comes from the book of "Clashians" (found in chapter zero, verse zero). They will ponder what it is that will keep grace radicals from going out and stealing, lying, or committing other sins, and think we're suggesting it's okay for people to go out and sin as much as they want. Whenever someone makes comments such as these, they have exposed their lack of understanding about God's grace and it is usually the result of being bound by the shackles of religious rules. Instead of *trying* to live by a code that was impossible (as Israel demonstrated), we now live by the ministry of the Spirit of God who abides in us.

The commandments are not our guide; *Jesus said the Spirit would be our guide* and lead us into all truth. From the beginning of the Bible, we find it is God who always wanted to be the guide. The only effective guidance the commandments could provide was to show people they were going around in circles while being hopelessly lost. Israel was too proud to stop and ask for directions but Professor Law would ultimately point them to the narrow gate of Christ and his righteousness, where their relationship with the good Professor would come to an end.

It is seemingly difficult for people to trust in grace (God) alone. Yet it is he alone who is our life, our accountability, our guide and teacher. We can now bear *his* fruit as the Spirit produces it through us, apart from law. If you mix law with grace, it may look good from a distance, but you'll just end up back at the tree of the knowledge of good and evil, where abiding in *thou shall not* will produce nothing but imitation, plastic (dead) fruit.

> "But the fruit of the Spirit is love, joy, peace, patience, kindness, goodness, faithfulness, gentleness, self-control; *against such things there is no law*" (Galatians 5:22–23). *Italics added.*

Notice it isn't the *fruits* of the Spirit. Don't fall into the fleshly trap of trying to produce each of the nine characters listed and turn it into a self-improvement rule book. Much like the old law, the *fruit* of the Spirit all comes together in the same package and is now a part of who you are with a new identity in Christ. This is so much lighter and easier when we trust his life within.

Faith Means Freedom

The Apostle Paul made the statement that if he proclaimed the gospel, it gave him no grounds for boasting. He then reveals the attitude he has taken on since receiving a new heart:

> "For though I am free from all, I have made myself a servant to all, that I might win more of them. To the Jews I became as a Jew, in order to win Jews. To those under the law I became as one under the law (though not being myself under the law) that I might win those under the law. To those outside the law I became as one outside the law (not being outside the law of God but under the law of Christ) that I might win those outside the law" (1 Corinthians

9:19–21).

He went on to say that he desired to be all things to all people in order to win some. In this liberty that comes from Christ, we are free to do what we want. Legalists will jump to the conclusion this means people will automatically have the intention of running around looking for sinful opportunities to see what they can "get away with." As God's grace and unconditional love becomes realized within a brand new heart, it can change what we want or desire. In fact, it is likely that once we begin to recognize the Christian life is all about *his* life in us, the struggles will begin to dissipate because the pressure is off. When an athlete is down to the final play of the game because time is running out, they will often choke because the pressure is too great. Sometimes it's called overtime, also known as sudden death. They know they have to make the play or they will lose. One's performance is usually greater when they can relax and be themselves without the pressure of "do or die."

> " 'All things are lawful,' but not all things are helpful. 'All things are lawful,' but not all things build up. Let no one seek his own good, but the good of his neighbor' " (1 Corinthians 10:23–24).

While we're free in Christ, not all choices are going to be helpful or profitable. That's why new covenant writers often encouraged believers to do the right thing and set a good example because *this is now who we are in him*. It's not to establish or maintain rightness with God, but *because* we're right with him. Love will not seek to benefit ourselves, but the well-being of those around us. In other words, exhortations regarding our outward living were meant for us to realize who we already are in Christ and to live from this new inward identity. How do we do that? Not by our own efforts of *trying*, but from *resting* in the source of life and power of the One who resides in us. Admittedly, after coming into the freedom of pure grace, I did begin using some four-letter words that had been typically absent from my vocabulary. Don't be overly concerned if this happens to you, for it is to be expected when grace begins to dominate your life. Words such as love, life, free, hope, gift, rest, and good news will naturally begin to manifest themselves from out of nowhere.

Our Holy Helper

Jesus did not leave us comfortless to try to figure out everything on our own. He sent us a Helper to lead, guide, and teach us in righteousness. There is no picture of the Holy Spirit hanging on the wall, so sometimes we have a hard time relating to him. But this shouldn't be the case, because he is just as caring, loving, and compassionate as Jesus, and the two are one with the Father.

> "These things I have spoken to you while I am still with you. But the Helper, the Holy Spirit, whom the Father will send in my name, he will teach you all things and bring to your remembrance all that I have said to you" (John 14:25-26).

Some will have the mindset that part of the work of the Holy Spirit is to convict people of their sins. In my earlier days of covenant confusion, I used to fall back on a Christian talking point by saying, "The Spirit will not condemn us of our sins, but he will convict us of our sins." Let's repent from that and change our thinking.

> "Nevertheless, I tell you the truth: it is to your advantage that I go away, for if I do not go away, the Helper will not come to you. But if I go, I will send him to you. And when he comes, he will convict the world concerning sin and righteousness and judgment: concerning sin, because they do not believe in me; concerning righteousness, because I go to the Father, and you will see me no longer; concerning judgment, because the ruler of this world is judged" (John 16:7-11).

Jesus just referenced three groups who are abiding in this world and summarized what conviction meant for all of them. First, unbelieving people (*they* do not believe in me). Second, believing people who are now considered righteous (*you* will see me no longer). Last and certainly least, the enemy (the ruler of this world is judged).

The Holy Spirit will *not* convict the world of its acts of *individual sins* because this is not the core problem. In this instance, Jesus is describing the *condition* of sin (noun) inherited from Adam. The real issue that needs to be addressed is the conviction of unbelief. On the other hand, the Holy Spirit will be there to convict believers of *righteousness* because Jesus conquered and rose from the dead. Those who are established in faith are described as righteous, not those pursuing works.

The very nature of your new identity in Christ will help you recognize when you've done something wrong. The ministry of the Spirit is not to point out the failure of sins, but to expose, convince, and bring a reminder that you are still a righteous child of God. He is called the Helper and Comforter, not the accuser, and he will reveal the strength of God which empowers you to participate in his miraculous way of life. Being receptive to this truth will help keep you from falling into the trap of guilt and condemnation.

The enemy who is called the accuser will attempt to prosecute charges against you. However, the Spirit of God brings the conviction or reminder that it is not you, but the ruler of this world who is judged. Jesus did not come to judge the world, but to save it (remember John 3:17-18). The Spirit will remind you of this truth that was spoken by Jesus, so listen for it. As for those who do not believe, they are "judged already."

The law increased sins while sacrifices brought a reminder of sins. The job of the Holy Spirit is quite different from that former ministry—it's not to convict people of sins that he remembers no more in a new and better covenant. It's to remind them they are righteous and holy, and that we can now live outwardly from this truth.

We have been living in a world where we work in order to receive. Money is the machine that makes this world system go around. Generally, if we don't work, we may not eat. We are naturally programmed to think this way and it can carry over into how we believe the Lord relates to us: "Now we have received not the spirit of the world, but the Spirit who is from God, that we might understand the things freely given us by God" (1 Corinthians 2:12).

God hasn't given us the spirit of this world that leads to fear. Instead, he gave us *his* Spirit so we would know the things *freely* given to us by God.

We can rest in that freedom.

(17) A NEW CREATION

A S SOMEONE WHO IS IN JESUS CHRIST, the real you went through a new birth of the spirit, a re-creation of sorts. Jesus spoke to Nicodemus about being born of the Spirit, and Peter and John also spoke of being born again, or born of God. It mainly refers to new life, to beget, or to father. We didn't work at doing something to cause our own birth. I know we refer to giving birth as labor, but it came from another source—the Giver of Life.

The words *new creation* in the following passage means to be formed from nothing, unused or newly made. God didn't just reshape you or improve you, he inwardly made you into something that wasn't there before, and old things have passed away in your spirit. We often use the phrase "passed away" referring to someone's death. That's what happened here; you died with Christ and were raised a new creature with a new identity.

> "Therefore, if anyone is in Christ, he is a new creation. The old has passed away; behold, the new has come. All this is from God, who through Christ reconciled us to himself and gave us the ministry of reconciliation; that is, in Christ God was reconciling the world to himself, not counting their trespasses against them, and entrusting to us the message of reconciliation" (2 Corinthians 5:17-19).

I used to think this passage meant the old things that passed away were all the bad choices we made, and the new things were the good "Christian" things we should do. I thought it was all up to me from now on. But *all this is from God*. In context of what Paul said leading up to this, it's easy to see he was referring to your inward person—the real you—meaning your spirit. Leading up to these verses, Paul had been comparing us as spirit beings living in a physical body. It is often said that we are "spirit, soul, and body." More accurately you *are* a spirit, you have a soul (mind, emotions), and you are living in a temporary, physical body. When the body ceases to function, you will depart from it and enter into a world that is even more real than this one. This physical world we live in was created from that world of the spirit we can't see.

I'm aware of various theological doctrines that will debate otherwise, but you simply can't have two natures within your spirit, with one being holy and the other being sinful. The Pharisees accused Jesus of such a thing, but a house divided against itself can't stand. People will often assume they have two natures because of the struggles they continue to encounter with the activity of sin. However, as believers we discover God exchanged death for life by taking away the sinful nature inherited from Adam, and replaced it with his righteous nature and all the good things associated with it—not the least of which is a supernatural, brand new life.

Unfortunately, the popular NIV translation has used the phrase "sinful nature" on occasion, which has caused confusion and would lead to contradictions if it were accurate. Fortunately, revisions have been made to this since 2011 and was changed to the word *flesh* in many instances, like nearly every other English Bible. The Greek word is *sarx* (Strong's G4561) and examples can be found in many places such as Romans 13:14 and Colossians 2:11. In Christ, you are no longer partnered or identified with a sinful nature—*you are a partaker of the divine nature* (see 2 Peter 1:4). You were born of God within the spirit of your inner being and you have a new heart that is not the producer of sin. Although *sarx* can be considered from more than one perspective, the word is clearly not defined as "sinful nature."

Paul said when the Spirit of God dwells in us, we are not in the flesh, but in the Spirit. Nonetheless, we battle against the ugly forces of sin through this thing called the flesh. Paul said nothing good dwells within the flesh. He spoke of the struggle in wanting to do what is good, but would sometimes end up doing the evil he did not want. He then follows with this from Romans 7:20: "Now if I do what I do not want, it is no longer I who do it, but sin that dwells within me." This is a real revelation and should be of great encouragement to us ... *it is no longer I who do it.* The sin he speaks of that dwells within him isn't referring to the inner man, but the mind and body (see Romans 7:22–23).

Paul would go on to conclude that it would be Jesus Christ who would deliver him from the "body" of death. Don't confuse the flesh with having a "sinful nature." This is why the Apostle John stated whoever is born of God cannot sin. It doesn't mean sinful actions can't occur, but it is not found in Christ who dwells inside the real you. He took sin away, and it doesn't abide alongside a nature of holiness—it's just not a part of who you are in him.

At the cross, Jesus became sin for us without committing one sinful act. Likewise, in him we became holy, apart from committing a single righteous act. Jesus became sin so that we could become the righteousness of God ... so here's a question: Is Jesus a sinner and does he have a sinful nature? The answer is no. Therefore, it will profit us to remember, *as he is, so also are we in this world* (see 1 John 4:17).

"Amen, Over and Out!"

Have you ever felt as though you had left a voicemail on the heavenly answering machine but the call was never returned? You can rest in knowing that you weren't being ignored. The enemy and possibly even religion had convinced you of being unworthy or undeserving. In fact, God is the one who called *you* and it may cause one to wonder how often he is ignored without us even realizing it. The Lord is so affectionately crazy about you and cares for you in a way that surpasses your understanding. When you become more aware of God's love and acceptance within you, prayer, meditation, and fellowship is something you'll find yourself in without even realizing it. What had formerly been a struggling monologue for me at times became meaningful conversation, often without me saying a word.

Since coming alive to grace, I have found myself spending less time in what would be considered prayer by religion's definition of "quiet time" or "devotion." For me it has become more of an ongoing awareness and appreciation of continuous fellowship and relationship throughout my day, instead of something like a long-distance phone call to the international space station. This is how it ought to be, because we are in union with God through Jesus Christ. It began to occur to me that I had spent much more time in prayer than I thought I did over the years. All those times I thought I was talking to myself throughout the day ... it turns out God was listening to every word.

"Hey God, Come Here for A Minute"

We've fallen into the dubious habit of thinking we need to invite God into our presence. Whether we're praying solo or in a group setting, various catch phrases are used asking God to show up or to pour out a special anointing. It can practically become law for people. I understand some believe this is necessary in order for the Lord to manifest or fall in special ways, but once again religion has it backwards because we were the invitee—invited into *his* presence and he is always where you are. I believe as we become more aware of this reality, it may result in a greater outward manifestation of this power that already abides within us.

Although it provides a buffer while you are thinking about what to say, my exhortation is to stop asking God to come. This "invitation rule" can develop a frame of mind that leads one to think if God can come, he can also depart after the gathering is over. Instead we should ask for a more significant realization that God has *already* provided his anointing that is not only upon us, but in us, and it doesn't come and go.

Some will say they know God never leaves, but inviting him is just a way of expressing they want more of him or they are helpless without him. First of all, in Christ you can't get more of God than you already possess, but it's certainly true we can do nothing without him. I would encourage you to simply say what you mean. Suppose you needed help moving a table, and imagine you and I are standing next to each other. If you were to say "Come here for a minute," my response would probably be "I'm already here." What you really meant to say is that you needed help moving a table.

For whatever reason, Christians often have a hard time digesting "Christ in you." The King is already in our midst by his Spirit, he lives *within* us and he never leaves (see John 14:16). Paul did not say God began a good work upon you, but *in* you (see Philippians 1:6). God has perfectly completed the work upon us, now he works in and through us by a life of faith. The gifts of the Holy Spirit will flow through yielded vessels as he wills, but the Spirit will never migrate for a period of time with the intention of periodically returning—he never vacates.

Rather than looking for ten steps on how to invite the Holy Spirit into a room, first see if you can discover scriptural instruction on this practice from a new covenant perspective. I think you'll have a hard time finding it. God isn't looking for a welcome mat at our doorstep, neither should we anxiously anticipate his RSVP every time we send out an invitation. Instead of telling God he is welcome to join us, we can simply say "thank you." His response will be "*you* are welcome."

As demonstrated through Jesus, God yearns to make the scene where religionists are less likely to be found. He has no boundaries and no limits. The notion that we need to create an acceptable atmosphere that is more conducive towards feeling the presence of the Holy Spirit is more of a mind game to convince ourselves of God's response to us. Our intentions are good, but God's presence won't be found with any greater intensity in a prayer meeting taking place in a church building than it will in a bar down the street. In a mixed covenant culture, religion has a way of trying to creep into our minds in the most unsuspecting ways. Recall the "legalism detector" provided back in the first chapter when religion was defined as "people trying to do something to get a response from God instead of resting in his response to us."

A Case of Mistaken Identity

Beware of Christian clichés which can lead to a mistaken identity. For example, when we call ourselves *followers* or *disciples* of Jesus, it's similar to carrying around false identification. You see, religion will coach you to be a follower of Jesus, but that won't be good enough unless you are a *faithful* follower. Considering that a follower is someone who literally follows another from one location to the next, we should ask specifically what a faithful follower is. It will be interpreted in a wide range of different ways. What may be considered faithful to one person is viewed quite differently by another. Being defined and identified in this manner becomes a trap the enemy can exploit in the lives of God's children.

"To follow" implies taking some sort of action of one's choosing. This isn't necessarily a bad thing, but the point is that it doesn't define you as a new creation in Christ because your identity is not based upon right *doing*, but right *being*. Those who were called followers of Jesus as he walked the earth would accompany him from place to place. You're not identified as just a *follower* of Jesus—you're a child of the living God being led by his Spirit. What's the difference? Check out a Greek lexicon and discover that to be "led" suggests being guided or carried, and it implies the Spirit of Life now leads by accompanying *you* (see Romans 8:14-15). He will be there to help direct your path, but regardless of which direction you decide to go, he will always be with you.

In the NASB, the Greek word *akoloutheo* appears dozens of times and is translated in English as: follow, followed, following and follows. The vast majority of these appear in the four books known as the gospels, and this is because it is referring to people who literally followed Jesus. There are a few occasions when English translations use a variation of the word "follow" in epistles from the apostles in the New Testament. These generally come from a different Greek word and it means *to imitate*. Although it can have a similar meaning, this is not the same as being a follower. I'm not trying to come down on people who insist on calling themselves followers of Jesus, but it's not an accurate description and it isn't part of your inheritance as a new creation.

We know those who followed Jesus during his earthly ministry would go wherever he went. It should cause one to ponder what the intended destination might be for the "followers" of today. I could've been a follower of Forrest Gump when he decided to run until the highway came to an end. Where Forrest would go, I would've followed as one who accompanied him. What happened when Forrest quit running? His band of followers had no idea what they should do next, much like the followers of Jesus after the crucifixion. Why? They ran into a brick wall where the "following" ceased at the cross, but they would soon relocate to being led by the Spirit of God. You're not a mere follower of Jesus as though you are lagging behind while trying to advance your position in order to get closer;

you are "in him" always and forever.

On the subject of being a disciple of Jesus, that won't be good enough either, because you'll be challenged to be a *dedicated* disciple. Just exactly what is a disciple? In the original language, a disciple is simply a pupil or student, nothing more. Jesus put it this way: "A disciple is not above his teacher, but everyone when he is fully trained will be like his teacher" (Luke 6:40).

Jesus clearly defined the unachievable goal for those who were under the law: Work diligently at becoming as perfect as he was through their own efforts. Ultimately, this would mean the need to count the cost and carry a cross—just as Jesus would do. This is not really meant to be the foundation for people to build anything that will last, but it's another example of Jesus ministering the heavy burden of the first covenant.

> "Whoever does not bear his own cross and come after me cannot be my disciple. For which of you, desiring to build a tower, does not first sit down and count the cost, whether he has enough to complete it? Otherwise, when he has laid a foundation and is not able to finish, all who see it begin to mock him, saying, 'This man began to build and was not able to finish' " (Luke 14:27–30).

Take a good look at what Jesus said right before this. Since a true disciple is supposed to become like the teacher, it meant giving up everything, including family. When Jesus said to carefully count the cost, he isn't requesting a denarius deposit from would-be followers and disciples. He is attempting to show how they couldn't cover the price necessary to complete the task at hand, and they would never be able to utter the words "it is finished." They may be able to get started, but only he would be able to finish the job by payment with his blood. This is what the word *redeem* means—to release by ransom or to buy away from. Jesus was elevating the law to show those who were under it they would need to look to him for righteousness, instead of themselves.

Next he summarized the entire *disciple of Jesus* movement that was taking place with this discouraging statement:

"So then, none of you can be My disciple who does not give up all his own possessions. Therefore, salt is good; but if even salt has become tasteless, with what will it be seasoned? It is useless either for the soil or for the manure pile; it is thrown out. He who has ears to hear, let him hear" (Luke 14:33-35 NASB).

By now, you ought to be able to recognize this as *law talk* from the Lord to the Jews who stood before him. Did these people have any clue as to what Jesus was talking about by carrying their own cross? Of course not. They couldn't even wrap their minds around Jesus rising from the dead, even though he stated it quite plainly. In fact, in the ninth chapter of Luke, right before Jesus told them they would need to carry their own cross, he said he would need to suffer, die and would rise again on the third day.

In the context of the disciples carrying their own cross, this statement followed: "Whoever tries to save their life will lose it" (see Luke 9:22-24). Yet we find whoever loses their life for the sake of Jesus will save it. Your life was lost (or killed) and is no longer your own because you were placed into Christ, you died with him and received *his* life (remember Galatians 2:20). We should not try to save ourselves and there is no need for us to do what Jesus did by suffering with our own cross. Whereas Jesus carried the cross once and for all, you and I would've been required to do it daily, much like the repeated animal sacrifices which could not take away sin.

In the tenth chapter of Matthew, Jesus said whoever does not take up their cross and follow after him, is not worthy of him—or not deserving, not having the same value. This was in the context of being his disciple, meaning to become just like Jesus through what one does. The truth is that everyone is undeserving of the title of *disciple* when it comes to being like Jesus and following his lead—doing everything perfectly and actually carrying a cross that brings redemption.

You'll find a vast array of interpretations about what Jesus meant by carrying "our" cross, but this wasn't hyperbole. People will often ask, "What did Jesus mean when he said we need to carry our cross?" I will make a radical suggestion that Jesus actually meant what he said, as he was attempting to show these people the futility of trying to be like the Teacher by following him to the end, and literally carrying their own physical cross in order to finish the redemptive work that needed to be done.

In addition to what has been stated, here is the clincher on why we know Jesus was speaking these things to people under the law and not believers who are now in Christ: There is *nothing* in new covenant writings from the apostles about us carrying our own cross. That's because there is *"the"* cross that only Jesus would be able to bear, and he did for us what we could not do for ourselves. The work he completed at his cross was more than enough. The vantage point we have by being positioned in a new covenant allows us to see that Jesus wasn't expecting us to carry a cross that only he could successfully endure. Jesus wasn't instructing future generations on how to be his disciple with a list of rigid requirements. Instead he was showing the Israelites of that time their inability to do so— attempting to be like him and paying their own debt. This is what the Lord wants us to learn from him: Anyone coming to Jesus who is exhausted and overwhelmed from religious labor will find rest for their souls.

> "Come to me, all who labor and are heavy laden, and I will give you rest. Take my yoke upon you, and learn from me, for I am gentle and lowly in heart, and you will find rest for your souls. For my yoke is easy, and my burden is light" (Matthew 11:28-30).

The discipleship demands of hating family and giving up everything lacks harmony with my *yoke is easy and my burden is light*. Why? You guessed it, two different covenants are being ministered at different times.

The main word for disciple in the Greek appears 246 times in the New Testament of the NASB (Strong's G3101). All of those references are found in the four books known as the gospels except for 26 which appear in the book of Acts. A significant clue as to why "disciple" is not part of your new identity in Christ is because the word doesn't appear *one single time* in New Testament writings after that. Take a timeout and think about that for a minute. If being a disciple were an integral part of the identity of a believer, one would think that Paul or another apostle would've used it at least once or twice to describe us in Christ. A disciple is simply a learner of the good news, which is a good thing to *do*, but it doesn't define who you *are*. It is not part of your spiritual DNA.

Michael C. Kapler

"But Jesus said all would know we are his disciples by our love for one another!" Not exactly. Jesus spoke this to *his* disciples in the thirteenth chapter of John as he addressed them as little children, a term of affection used by a teacher to their disciples. He told them to love one another *as he loved them*. He was speaking to his pupils who were with him and had been learning from him.

Keep in mind, of all the disciples following Jesus, he had earlier appointed twelve as apostles (messengers). In Matthew 28:19, Jesus commissioned the eleven to go and make disciples of all nations. To *make disciples* here means the action of teaching others. The word *nations* is where the word Gentile comes from. The startling revelation in what Jesus said when sending the apostles was that they would teach and proclaim the message to those outside of Israel. Their goal wasn't to try to "sell" Jesus to the world and hope they would be rewarded with a "great commission." *Jesus did not commission people to go and finish the job he started, he sent them to tell others the work is finished.* The manifestation of miracles is not meant to be the directive, but is an offshoot of that message. Signs would *follow* the teaching of the good news of the finished work of Christ.

We find John the Baptist had disciples, and in the book of Acts, the apostles had disciples too. These were pupils learning from a teacher, but it did not necessarily make them direct followers or disciples of Jesus.

Surrender and Give Your All?

Christian religion that is based on a covenant combination will announce how God sent Jesus to redeem humanity, but watch out for the "if's." For example, you'll hear that God will bring light and life "if" you give yourself completely to him. God will bless and respond to you "if" you are willing to surrender everything to him, even the things we hold nearest and dearest. These generic talking points sound correct and preach real smooth, but it puts *you* back in the spotlight where Jesus should be standing.

Just exactly what is meant by surrendering everything and giving your all? Jesus explained it pretty well to the Jews under the first covenant and it boiled down to the impossibility of maintaining perfection. Preachers using these types of conditional catch phrases may attempt to imply a few things, but generally they will leave it to your imagination on what it means to "surrender and give your all." That's because it's just more religious double-talk that will mean a thousand different things to a thousand different people. Many side dishes from Scripture will be placed before you in the attempt to make their case, but the all-you-can-eat verse buffet isn't necessarily the tastiest when the combinations aren't compatible with the main course.

In Christ, we *submit* ourselves to God and his righteousness, meaning "to place under or subject to"—something the Jewish people did not do under the previous covenant (see Romans 10:3). Our submission to this *gift* is quite different from the legalistic message that leads to the wrong question of "what must I do to surrender everything."

When others attempt to use words such as *dedicated* and *faithful* to determine your identity as a Christian, just remember how God demonstrated his love, dedication and faithfulness *to you*. He is the only true promise keeper. He is the one who surrendered everything and we can't pay him back, nor is he expecting us to do so. If the good news is validated because of our promises to God or to others, that would be bad news for all of us.

The song says, "Though none go with me, still I will follow." Really? Here is the bottom line on the subject of mistaken identity: If you think the ultimate goal of a Christian is to be a committed follower and disciple of everything Jesus taught, be sure to take your altar out of storage, give up all your possessions and obey every commandment from the law to perfection.

Walking in New Life

As we start sharing a gospel without phony additives, preservatives, or artificial colors and flavors, just watch how people are attracted to it. I recall an occasion when I was having lunch at a restaurant with my pastor and a couple of friends, sharing and discussing this good news of God's grace—the gospel that we went without for so many years of our Christian life. We had talked for an hour when I noticed the middle-aged couple at a nearby table. It turned out they had been within earshot of the many things we were talking about, and I can assure you we were discussing free grace and God's love like most people have never heard it before. It was probably my imagination, but after our conversation I was pretty sure I saw leftover baskets full of bread and fish scattered throughout the restaurant. It was that good.

As we got up to leave, the woman from the table turned and asked if we all went to the same church. They were new in town and were looking for somewhere to attend. As we were going out the door, it was as if the Lord gave me an elbow and said, "See what happens when people hear *my* true gospel?" The world is hungry for this, and they should have it. God paid for them to have it.

Do you truly trust in what he accomplished for you? If you are one of the many who have only been fed lifeless religion or church without Jesus and have missed the gospel or failed to grasp its message, let me encourage you. It's not that you have to recite a specific sinner's prayer, but we *are* encouraged to vocalize a profession of faith. When you believe it with the heart, the mouth will follow. There is just one confession or agreement, and that is a confession of the Lord Jesus Christ. You can say it out loud in your own words, but if you need help getting started, here's a sample:

> Father, I confess Jesus Christ is Lord, and I believe you raised him from the dead. I call upon his name to save me. Thank you that his blood has brought me complete forgiveness. I place my trust in you, and I receive the gift of new life and righteousness you have given through the cross.

Welcome to the New and Everlasting Covenant found in your best friend, the eternal God and Savior, Jesus Christ!

EPILOG

HERE ARE SOME CLOSING THOUGHTS I hope you will carry with you, because it is your current reality in him: You were killed, placed into Christ at the cross, perfected and declared righteous, holy, and blameless. You've been exposed eternally to unconditional love that keeps no record of wrong and does not count sins against us, because in this New Covenant, God remembers our sins no more and isn't dealing with us according to our sins. Forgiveness from God isn't something that occurs repeatedly when we're "sorry" or because we are willing to forgive; rather it is a completed work that happened with one bloody sacrifice.

I realize you may be having trouble wrapping your mind around certain aspects of what has been stated about the commandments, the covenants and the gospel. The quick take-away is this: The commandments engraved on stones were called the tablets of the covenant. Which covenant? The *first one* God made with Israel that came to an end at the cross. Those commandments were given to provide people an opportunity to put forth their best effort through their own works; they were not designed to bring improvement or help to regulate sin, but to show man couldn't achieve anything apart from God. It came with a different assurance than we have with Jesus—*it was guaranteed to fail.* There is nothing wrong with the law, but it is not our solution. Instead it points us to the answer of Jesus Christ.

Those commands that brought death and condemnation, along with the hundreds of others that came with them, were replaced with a new ministry of the Spirit of God as a result of the accomplished work of Jesus Christ. Our roots are connected directly to Him working in us and through us. Instead of a mindset focused on "thou shall not," the Spirit of God exudes new life allowing us to bear his fruit apart from any commandment of the law. For those still clinging to the requirement of keeping *some* of those laws, they must answer a question that requires very specific answers: Which laws were removed and which ones are to be kept? One can't talk in generalities on this subject, we need to know *exactly* what has been crossed off the list and what has not. Who will be elected the "president" of Christianity that has the power to use a line item veto? Hopefully you can begin to see the flawed approach in thinking the commandments from the first covenant could be conveniently broken up to be applied as we see fit. They came as a package, and thankfully for us they ended in the same way.

If there is *any* activity you think needs to be performed in order to receive or maintain God's acceptance, forgiveness, blessings or fellowship, then salvation should be defined as something that is earned, not a gift. If right standing with God comes through any work or religious exercise that you must perform, execute or observe, then the grace of God is nullified and Christ died needlessly (remember Galatians 2:21). In other words, you would be on your own and faith would have to be considered a myth. Religious tradition has gotten it backwards—faith doesn't come by our good works and improved performance, it comes by hearing the truth of God's Word, and then it works through unconditional love that keeps no record of wrong. It's God's love to the extreme! As righteous people, we live by the law of faith, which is very different from religious rules related to our efforts through various dogmas with roots connected to the law of works (remember Romans 3:27).

If we think too hard, things like resting, believing, and faith become difficult in our minds, and we'll find ourselves "trying harder" to abide in them. It wasn't meant to be that way, because abiding in Jesus doesn't involve effort on your part. He will simply do it through you. It takes no effort on our part to abide in a room while relaxing on the couch. Likewise, we now abide and rest in Jesus Christ, and his Spirit will be the one to produce the fruitful results of love, joy, peace, patience, kindness, goodness, faithfulness, gentleness, and self-control.

You will know you're getting the gospel right when the source of persecution comes less from doubters and unbelievers, while increasing from religious people. As a recovering covenant clasher myself, I urge you to leave behind the insurmountable, unattainable, and impossible rules that only slow you down. Repent by changing the way you have thought about God and how you may have related to him through a system of works that came through various kinds of law or other religious sources. Believe the good news of grace and truth that is realized through Jesus Christ. Never forget ... God isn't angry with you!

Covenant Clarification—the List

Here is a short list to summarize some of the differences between the two covenants:

Old: Counted trespasses against us.
New: Not counting our sins against us (2 Corinthians 5:19).

Old: Brought guilt, condemnation and death.
New: Brought life, removed guilt and condemnation (Romans 8:1-2).

Old: Continuous consciousness of sins (a guilty conscience).
New: Delivered from the consciousness of sins (Hebrews 10:1-2).

Old: Reminded of sins.
New: Sins remembered no more (Hebrews 10:17).

Old: Wrath.
New: Peace (Romans 5:1).

Old: Weak and useless, the law made nothing perfect.
New: Perfection through a better hope and guarantee of Jesus (Hebrews 7:18-22).

Old: Depended upon a person's behavior.
New: Depends upon Jesus Christ (John 14:6).

Old: Sin abounded.

New: Grace abounded much more (Romans 5:20).

Old: Try harder to bring change.
New: God reconciled us through exchange (Colossians 1:22).

Old: Caused sin to increase.
New: Sin taken away once and for all (1 John 3:5; Hebrews 10:10).

Old: Heavy and burdensome.
New: Easy and light (Matthew 11:30).

Old: Unable to establish righteousness through works.
New: The gift of God's righteousness received by faith (Romans 3:21–22).

Old: Separated, far off, excluded, strangers.
New: Accepted, brought near, fellow citizens (Ephesians 2:13).

Old: Dead in sins.
New: Alive in Christ (Ephesians 2:5).

Old: One seeks after God.
New: God seeks you (Luke 15:4, 8–9, 20; John 15:16).

Old: Love by command with all your heart and strength.
New: We love because we realize he first loved us (1 John 4:19).

Old: Not qualified.
New: God qualified us (Colossians 1:12).

Old: Forgiveness temporary, incomplete.
New: Forgiven completely (Colossians 2:13).

Old: Unholy people.
New: Made holy and blameless (Ephesians 1:4; Colossians 1:22).

Old: Walk in the flesh.
New: Walk in the Spirit (Romans 8:9; Galatians 5:16, 18).

Old: Blessings were conditional.
New: Blessings are freely given by his Spirit (1 Corinthians 2:12).

Old: Death and darkness.
New: Life and light (2 Timothy 1:10; 1 Thessalonians 5:5).

Old: Exclusively for Israel and temporary.
New: Available to all and everlasting (Romans 3:29-30).

Old: People at fault.
New: People perfected (Hebrews 10:14).

Old: Aroused sinful passions.
New: Teaches us to deny ungodliness (Titus 2:12).

Old: The law was not of faith.
New: The law of faith (Romans 3:27).

Old: Ended with Christ.
New: Established by Christ (Hebrews 8:6).

Old: Yoke of bondage.
New: Liberty (Galatians 5:1; James 1:25).

Old: Good and once had glory.
New: Better and more glorious (2 Corinthians 3:7-8).

Old: Many sacrifices.
New: One sacrifice (Hebrews 9:12, 10:12).

Old: Fear and torment.
New: Love and peace (Ephesians 6:23).

ABOUT THE AUTHOR

MICHAEL C. KAPLER works in the communications industry and has a 20-year background in Christian radio ministry. He has co-hosted the weekly *Growing in Grace* podcast since 2005, openly admits to never having attended Seminary or Bible College, and considers The Three Stooges to be among the greatest philosophers in human history.

In both this book and in his podcasts, Mike (known by many as Kap) challenges some traditional religious mindsets with a serious approach alongside a clever sense of humor and quick wit, bringing a unique, simple perspective towards gaining a fresh understanding of the gospel of grace.

To download podcasts, visit GrowinginGrace.org.

Made in United States
Orlando, FL
27 October 2023

38306103R00127